▶ Participation, Citizenship and Intergenerational
Relations in Children and Young People's Lives

DOI: 10.1057/9781137379702.0001

Other Palgrave Pivot Titles

Jonathan Grix: Leveraging Legacies from Sports Mega-Events: Concepts and Cases

Edward Webb: Media in Egypt and Tunisia: From Control to Transition?

Dayan Jayatilleka: The Fall of Global Socialism: A Counter-Narrative From the South

Linda Lawrence-Wilkes and Lyn Ashmore: The Reflective Practitioner in Professional Education

Anna-Brita Stenström: Teenage Talk: From General Characteristics to the Use of Pragmatic Markers in a Contrastive Perspective

Divya Wodon, Naina Wodon, and Quentin Wodon: Membership in Service Clubs: Rotary's Experience

Robert C. Robinson: Justice and Responsibility—Sensitive Egalitarianism

Alison Heron Hruby and Melanie Landon-Hays (editors): Digital Networking for School Reform: The Online Grassroots Efforts of Parent and Teacher Activists

R. A. Houston: The Coroners of Northern Britain c. 1300–1700

Christina Slade: Watching Arabic Television in Europe: From Diaspora to Hybrid Citizens

Fred E. Knowles: The Indian Law Legacy of Thurgood Marshall

Louisa Hadley: Responding to Margaret Thatcher's Death

Kylie Mirmohamadi: The Digital Afterlives of Jane Austen: Janeites at the Keyboard

Rebeka L. Maples: The Legacy of Desegregation: The Struggle for Equality in Higher Education

Stijn Vanheule: Diagnosis and the DSM: A Critical Review

James DeShaw Rae: Analyzing the Drone Debates: Targeted Killing, Remote Warfare, and Military Technology

Torben Bech Dyrberg: Foucault on the Politics of Parrhesia

Bernice M. Murphy: The Highway Horror Film

Jolene M. Sanders: Women in Narcotics Anonymous: Overcoming Stigma and Shame

Bruce E. Bechtol, Jr.: North Korea and Regional Security in the Kim Jong-un Era: A New International Security Dilemma

Patrick Alan Danaher, Andy Davies, Linda De George-Walker, Janice K. Jones, Karl J. Matthews, Warren Midgley, Catherine H. Arden, and Margaret Baguley: Contemporary Capacity-Building in Educational Contexts

Margaret Baguley, Patrick Alan Danaher, Andy Davies, Linda De George-Walker, Janice K. Jones, Karl J. Matthews, Warren Midgley and Catherine H. Arden: Educational Learning and Development: Building and Enhancing Capacity

Marian Lief Palley and Howard A. Palley: The Politics of Women's Health Care in the United States

Nikhilesh Dholakia and Romeo V. Turcan: Toward a Metatheory of Economic Bubbles: Socio-Political and Cultural Perspectives

Tommi A. Vuorenmaa: Lit and Dark Liquidity with Lost Time Data: Interlinked Trading Venues around the Global Financial Crisis

DOI: 10.1057/9781137379702.0001

palgrave▶pivot

Participation, Citizenship and Intergenerational Relations in Children and Young People's Lives: Children and Adults in Conversation

Edited by

Joanne Westwood
University of Central Lancashire, UK

Cath Larkins
University of Central Lancashire, UK

Dan Moxon
People Dialogue and Change Ltd, UK

Yasmin Perry
University of Central Lancashire, UK

Nigel Thomas
University of Central Lancashire, UK

palgrave
macmillan

DOI: 10.1057/9781137379702.0001

First published 2014 by
PALGRAVE MACMILLAN

Palgrave Macmillan in the UK is an imprint of Macmillan Publishers Limited, registered in England, company number 785998, of Houndmills, Basingstoke, Hampshire RG21 6XS.

Palgrave Macmillan in the US is a division of St Martin's Press LLC, 175 Fifth Avenue, New York, NY 10010.

Palgrave Macmillan is the global academic imprint of the above companies and has companies and representatives throughout the world.

Palgrave® and Macmillan® are registered trademarks in the United States, the United Kingdom, Europe and other countries.

ISBN: 978–1–137–37971–9   EPUB
ISBN: 978–1–137–37970–2   PDF
ISBN: 978–1–137–37969–6   Hardback

A catalogue record for this book is available from the British Library.

A catalog record for this book is available from the Library of Congress.

www.palgrave.com/pivot

DOI: 10.1057/9781137379702

Contents

DOI: 10.1057/9781137379702.0001

List of Figures

Foreword

The right to self-determination is the core principle of human rights discourse, through which civil society strives to realise all its other rights. Recognising that children's participation has its roots in human rights law, Richard Farson (1974, p. 27) writes, 'The issue of self determination is at the heart of children's liberation. It is, in fact, the only issue, a definition of the entire concept'. It is also clearly articulated in Article 12 of the UNCRC, which implies that it is through meaningful participation that children can demand, access and secure all their other rights to survival, protection and development. It is a process that empowers children to negotiate with duty bearers to determine the quality and nature of the services and infrastructure that is provided to them (Committee on the Rights of the Child, 2009).

The chapters in this very timely volume clearly reflect an ideological position that views children as subjects, as agents of change who have a right to exercise the power of their agency to transform their political, economic and socio-cultural realities. The topics cover three major areas – that of protagonism of children, of intergenerational relationships and key aspects of information management by children.

While the implications of a paradigm shift from viewing children as passive beneficiaries to that of holders of rights are presented with varying degrees of clarity, the recognition that it needs critical reflection – in the prevalent construct of childhood and of children's agency – comes through very clearly in the well-argued chapters. While

DOI: 10.1057/9781137379702.0003

attempting to place children in the centre, several of the articles review how children are impacted upon by their contexts and at the same time how they are also able to transform their contexts, provided they have the appropriate information and structures to have real impacts.

The chapters discuss a wide range of highly pertinent issues that include the potential of children to generate knowledge; expectations about the rigour, validity and ownership of children's research; and access of children to policy spaces where their voices are not only heard, but have the power to influence and shape policy and practise. Special emphasis is placed on children who are most marginalised, with an attention to power relations between adults and children – both within the community and within a 'research' setting, critiquing the traditional hierarchies and the implications of children's research on empowerment and social justice. It is within this larger context that the topic of children and research is examined through different lenses – with a good balance of young persons, activists and academics putting forth their innovative experiences, thought-provoking reviews and models.

When children and young person's engagement with research is seen as an integral aspect of their protagonism and their participation in society, the facilitative agencies have to factor in all the backward and forward linkages that are essential for it to have real and sustainable impact. Such a process will have to take into account the personhood of children, their heterogeneous composition, their multiple realities and the factors and structures that enable or affect their sustained involvement.

As a new discipline, children's research will have to develop its ethics within a children's rights-based ideology. Hence, the issues raised in these chapters related to de-mystification of research; coexistence of children- and adult-led research where children are viewed as a group capable of generating rigorous knowledge and critical reflection; and the impact of children's research on the discipline of childhood studies – all of these require deep reflection and systematic exploration. This volume is a very significant step forward in this direction.

Kavita Ratna
Director-Advocacy,
The Concerned for Working Children

DOI: 10.1057/9781137379702.0003

Acknowledgements

This edited collection has been a truly collaborative enterprise and emerged as a result of the commitment of the authors to develop their research presentations at the ICRYNet 2012 conference into fully fledged peer and young person reviewed chapters. Our editorial comments were always warmly received and we appreciate the efforts and time our authors dedicated to this. The editorial team worked closely with several children and young people who contributed to the writing and editing of this unique book. We are immensely proud of their contributions and delighted that they gave up their time and energy to this important task. Thanks are also owed to two research interns Charlotte Connolly and Sonia Kaur Virk who worked on the conference team in September 2012. Mark Barlow and Faith Matunda were involved in the University of Central Lancashire's undergraduate research internship scheme (URIS) and assisted the editorial team during the summer of 2013. The editorial team would also like to thank Rebecca Nowell and Sarah Lusher who were involved in the University of Central Lancashire's Young Researchers programme in August 2013 for their assistance with the preparation of the bibliography.

The authors are donating 50% of the royalties from the sale of this book to The Children's Participation Fund.

DOI: 10.1057/9781137379702.0004

Notes on Contributors

Paulina Billett is an associate lecturer at La Trobe University, Australia. She has a particular interest in youth studies in a rural context. She has presented and published articles on youth social capital, ethics in youth research and youth space and place, both nationally and internationally. Paulina has worked extensively with young people, and was a youth development officer for Community Links Wollondilly in Australia.

Anne Crowley is a policy and research consultant and honorary lecturer in the School of Social Sciences at Cardiff University. Anne has recently completed her doctoral studies looking at the impact of children's participation on policy making in the context of devolution in Wales. Anne is a member of the National Independent Advocacy Board which advises the Welsh Government on the development of advocacy services for children and young people. She co-edited the most recent 'alternative' report on progress in implementing the United Nations Convention on the Rights of the Child in Wales, *Stop, look, listen: the road to realising children's rights in Wales*.

Amanda Hatton is a qualified social worker and worked for a number of years as an education social worker and as a case holder for a youth offending project. Research undertaken for her doctoral thesis was based on the participation of children and young people, using creative arts and methods. She is currently working for a local authority as a senior staff development officer in a safeguarding children's training team, delivering multi-agency training, and is senior lecturer in childhood studies at Sheffield Hallam University, United Kingdom.

Martin Hughes is Chartered and HCPC registered psychologist and associate fellow of the British Psychological Society, and is a member of the Association of Educational Psychologists and the British Psychological Society. Martin taught in a secondary school for five years and since training in 1988 has been recognised as a chartered psychologist. Martin currently works part-time for Sheffield City Council as a senior educational psychologist and at the University of Sheffield, United Kingdom, where he is a lecturer in educational psychology and acting do-director, Doctorate of Educational and Child Psychology (DEdCPsy).

Vicky Johnson is a principal research fellow in the Education Research Centre at the University of Brighton. For the past twenty years she has been a practitioner researcher and manager in international non-governmental organisations and has carried out research and training in collaboration with UN organisations, local and national government and civil society organisations in the UK and internationally. Her research interests lie in the areas of: children and young people's participation; socio-ecological and socio-cultural theory; intergenerational dynamics and inclusion. Her role in the education research centre includes: teaching international and comparative education, inclusion and community engagement; encouraging learning and research across the school of education; understanding how to monitor and maximise impact; and encouraging international research partnerships.

Victoria Jupp-Kina is a qualified social worker with research and practice experience both in the United Kingdom and in Brazil. Victoria is a lecturer in Social Work in the School of Education, Social Work and Community Education at the University of Dundee in Scotland. Victoria's work focuses on international social work and community development and she has a particular interest in the connection between participation and sustainable community development.

Lucinda Kerawalla is a lecturer with the Open University, United Kingdom. She is a socio-cultural psychologist and her research interests include exploring the multivoiced nature of child-led research. She is also interested in technology enhanced learning interactions both inside and outside the classroom.

Cath Larkins is Co-director of The Centre for Children and Young People's Participation and a senior research fellow at the University of Central Lancashire. She was coordinator of Different Voices in Global Conversations, the international conference for children and young people that ran in parallel to ICYRNet 2012. She has worked as a participation facilitator for more than 15 years and writes about children's citizenship. She focuses particularly on participatory action research that supports marginalised children and young people to try to bring about changes in their lives, communities and the services they use. She is a member of the Eurochild advisory group on participatory methods for inclusion.

Siân Lucas is a lecturer in the School of Applied Social Sciences at the University of Stirling. Siân is ESRC sponsored Doctoral Candidate at the University of Salford, UK and HCPC registered social worker, with previous experience in Children's Services. Her research interests include: the delivery of social welfare services for non-English speakers, in particular the ways that children contribute through language and cultural brokering. Siân has won two ESRC awards: Internship at the Welsh Government and Overseas Institutional Visit to study child language brokering and immigration at the University of California, Los Angeles.

Samia Michail is a principal researcher in the Social Justice Unit of UnitingCare Children, Young People and Families. She has particular experience designing participatory research methodologies for working with children and young people that recognise and facilitate their agency and contribution to knowledge. Samia has published on research methods with young carers, and students with challenging behaviours in relation to school suspension. In 2011 she implemented the first child-led research program in Australia with children and young people living in disadvantaged communities.

Dan Moxon is Director of People, Dialogue and Change, a capacity-building and consultancy organisation that provides support for organisations in the area of youth participation and youth engagement, and associate director of The Centre for Children and Young People's Participation. Dan is regarded as an expert practitioner in the field of youth participation, with over 15 years of experience in the children, families and young people's sector. He has led work on behalf of the UK Youth Parliament, The Department of Health, Government Office North West and many other organisations. He provided support and

DOI: 10.1057/9781137379702.0005

co-ordination for the children and young people's international conference Different Voices in Global Conversations in 2012.

Roshni K. Nuggehalli is a freelance development professional. Roshni was formerly assistant director of The Concerned for Working Children where she managed the research, advocacy and communications department, including child-led research. She worked on issues of child labour, juvenile justice and children's information management and advocacy and was also involved in participatory monitoring and evaluation processes. A graduate of Purdue University in the United States, she holds a master's degree in human dimensions of natural resources.

Yasmin Perry is a programme lead for several routes into School Nursing at the University of Central Lancashire, United Kingdom. She trained as an adult and children's nurse and latterly as a school nurse and practice teacher in the community. Yasmin has experience of conducting research looking at young people's perceptions of School Health Services. She is a member of the National Forum of School Health Educators and academic advisor for the North West School Nurse Benchmarking Group. Yasmin was part of the ICYRNet 2012 international conference committee where she worked with the young people's planning group.

Nigel Thomas is a professor of childhood and youth research at the University of Central Lancashire. Nigel's research with children and young people includes child welfare, children's rights and theories of childhood, with a particular focus on children and young people's participation. He has worked with children in care, young carers, school pupils and members of youth councils, using a range of innovative methods. He is co-director and co-founder of The Centre for Children and Young People's Participation. Until recently he was co-editor of the journal *Children & Society*, and is now chair of the editorial board.

Joanne Westwood is a senior lecturer in social work at the University of Central Lancashire, United Kingdom, and is co-director of The Centre for Children and Young People's Participation. Joanne is a qualified social worker and worked in advocacy and participation programmes for several years. She has carried out extensive research and evaluation projects about the lives and experiences of vulnerable children and young people.

DOI: 10.1057/9781137379702.0005

1

Introduction

Westwood, Larkins, Moxon, Perry and Thomas

Abstract: *ICRYNet, an interdisciplinary research network concerned with children's and young people's participation, held their second conference in 2012 at The University of Central Lancashire in Preston UK. Over 200 academics, practitioners and children's rights advocates, together with groups of children and young people from across the globe discussed, debated and decided upon new ways of connecting with each other. The chapter introduces the highlights from these "Global Conversations" which are captured in this book. The chapter describes how children, young people and adults joined forces to develop new ways of working together producing a website (DVIGC.COM), a participation toolkit, and this volume of research papers covering three key areas: Participation and Citizenship, Spaces of Intergenerational Relations and Children and Young People as Researchers.*

Joanne Westwood, Cath Larkins, Dan Moxon, Yasmin Perry and Nigel Thomas. *Participation, Citizenship and Intergenerational Relations in Children and Young People's Lives: Children and Adults in Conversation.* Basingstoke: Palgrave Macmillan. DOI: 10.1057/9781137379702.0006.

In recent decades there has been a major growth of interest in research about and with children and young people. One recent manifestation of this was the creation in 2008 of the International Childhood and Youth Research Network (ICYRNet). This network promotes the inter-disciplinary study of children and young people, in order to further awareness and understanding of issues that affect their well-being. In 2012 The Centre for Children and Young People's Participation at the University of Central Lancashire hosted ICYRNet's second international conference on the theme 'Children, Young People and Adults: Extending the Conversation,' which attracted more than 200 delegates from all over the world. A unique feature of the conference was that it ran alongside an international gathering of children and young people, planned by children and young people, on the theme 'Young Citizens: Different Voices in Global Conversations.' The young people's planning group and the conference organising committee worked in partnership to deliver these two events in collaboration. The two events were hugely successful; in addition to several, varied opportunities for debates and discussions about research with children and young people, we saw presentations on many innovative projects about and with children and young people as co-researchers as well as participants.

Working with a group of undergraduate research interns funded by UCLan, the local organising committee working with Joshua Buckley developed a conference website, http://www.dvigc.com/ . During the summer of 2013 Mark Barlow worked with us to update and revise the website, and you will find references to the website throughout this book. The website provides additional visual and audio materials linked to several chapters in the book, as well as information about the presentations and activities at the conference. In addition, as part of the work for the conference Charlotte Connolly developed a toolkit for young people's participation in conferences. This toolkit draws on the experiences of developing the 'Different Voices in Global Conversations' event to provide guidance for future conference organisers on participa-tory methods and approaches, with insights into the different stages of planning, organising and delivery and highlighting key areas of success that may be replicated in other events. Sonia Kaur Virk developed and implemented several interactive evaluation activities for participants to feedback to the conference and young people's planning committee their thoughts and views about a range of elements of the conference. The evaluation report and the aforementioned conference participation

DOI: 10.1057/9781137379702.0006

toolkit are both available on the website http://www.dvigc.com/participation-toolkit-and-evaluation/. DVIGC.com is also open for new contributions and acts as a platform through which children and young people and the adults working with them on participatory research can share their findings, views and experiences (http://www.dvigc.com/young-people-conference/).

After the conference, the conference organising committee and the young people's planning group seized the opportunity to continue the ground-breaking 'global conversations' and proposed this edited collection of work. Young people were involved in contributing their critique of academic debates on participation – first at the conference and now through these chapters. During the preparation of the book, members of the editorial team met regularly with young people from three different groups and devised creative ways of exploring the chapters with them. Details of this process can be found within the opening chapters of each part of the book.[1] Author feedback was co-created by the young people and the editorial team, a collaboration which bridges the knowledge divide among young people, practitioners, students and academics. In this way we have produced a book for all of us, co-creating a space which is challenging, dynamic and takes debates about participation and citizenship forward in an inclusive manner. Our aim in working this way has been to set new standards for intergenerational dialogue through which children and young people can inform and shape the knowledge base about them, and guide the way adult researchers work and understand their lives.

Citizenship, participation and intergenerational relations

Citizenship is a contested concept, defined both as a status and as a set practice that enables and outlines the distribution of resources in a given political unit (Isin and Turner, 2007; Turner, 1993). It can be seen as a set of building blocks – rights, responsibilities, respect/recognition, participation and inclusion (Lister, 2007; Delanty, 2000). Legal or social practices connected with formal political institutions tend to dominate understandings of citizenship. This book, however, focuses on the practices in everyday lives through which children and young people enact citizenship by creating, transforming and challenging distributions of

DOI: 10.1057/9781137379702.0006

cultural and economic resources and social justice, for themselves and for others.

Children and young people do not of course act alone. Adults too are social actors actively engaged in negotiating, receiving, contributing to or limiting the achievement of rights, responsibilities, respect/recognition participation and inclusion for themselves and for other adults, children and young people. Citizenship then can usefully be seen as relational and intergenerational, reflecting the interdependence of adults and children and young people (Cockburn, 2013).

Our intergenerational focus (Alanen, 2009) in this book is the interactions between two social categories – adults, and children and young people. But, as the term 'children and young people' suggests, there are of course many differences within each of these generational categories and these social positions intersect with other social experiences like gender, race and class. Taking a relational focus, however, enables us to study childhood and adulthood as processes rather than children and adults as entities (Alanen, 2009).

Participation is central to citizenship (McGinley & Grieve, 2010) and is the core of intergenerational practice studies in this book. Hart (1992) equated movement upwards on a ladder of participation as movement towards citizenship. This hierarchical understanding has however been challenged (Shier, 2001; Treseder, 1997). Participation can be seen as generally 'taking part in an activity or specifically ... taking part in decision-making' (Thomas, 2007, p. 199). A majority world perspective (Mason & Bolan, 2010) widens this to include contributing to self, family and community. In some European definitions, however, participation initiatives remain as attempts to 'reinforce the connection between young people and public life' (Loncle, 2008, p. 37).

Tisdall (2010) however cautions that participation should be seen as a process of governance and not simply engagement in representative government. Participation may also be seen in children's involvement in the explicit and concealed decisions about 'routines, structures and interests that affect children' (Alderson, 2010, p. 94). These struggles for definition of participation echo the different understandings of citizenship, as both are then concerned with the spaces in which participation or other actions associated with citizenship take place, such as formal structures, civil society, family relationships or friendship groups. In whatever formal or informal, invited or created space, participation is a relational process through which children and young people

DOI: 10.1057/9781137379702.0006

communicate or take action with others and with resources to try to bring about change.

This book is divided into three parts, based on the themes from the ICYRNet conference:

▶ Part I: Participation and citizenship
▶ Part II: Spaces of intergenerational relations
▶ Part III: Children and young people as researchers

In the opening chapter Roshni Nuggehalli introduces us to the transformational potential which child-led research has for community and cultural change, drawing on examples of work undertaken by children in India. In these examples we can see how children's perspectives shaped and influenced the direction and impact of their research. The importance of distinguishing between children and young people as rights holders and trainee citizens is also a key issue. Nuggehalli reminds us that as academics and practitioners we have a responsibility to inform the theoretical dimensions of the discipline of childhood studies and support a shift towards a protagonist- and rights-based ideology. Her chapter concludes with a series of questions which challenge us to engage with this paradigm shift.

Part I of the book focuses on the theme of participation and the ways in which it can be made meaningful and result in change. Members of Preston Youth Council (PYC) worked with Yasmin Perry and Cath Larkins to write the introductory chapter to this section. Their chapter ties in Nuggehalli's work with that of Crowley, Hatton and Jupp-Kina and their own experiences. They reflect on the differences between approaches to participation in different locations and point to the need for further research on participation to explore the influence of environments, backgrounds, confidence levels and emotions, to pick apart the different roles children and young people engage in and the factors that influence whether or not change occurs as a result.

Anne Crowley continues the theme introduced by Roshni Nuggehalli, beginning her chapter with a discussion of what participation means for children and young people and reminding us that the realisation of rights to participate depends on solid political support if it is to move beyond tokenism. In this sense, whilst there has been progress, there is still a long journey ahead. Crowley argues that it is not simply a question of defining participatory approaches but also of evaluating their impact. She draws on four case studies from the United Kingdom and India and

DOI: 10.1057/9781137379702.0006

an international panel to explore the problems of measuring the impact of participation on children and young people's lives and relationships, and on policies and services. Utilising a range of research methods, she interrogates the processes of participatory work with children, young people and adults. Her contribution, together with Nuggehalli's, shows how the involvement of children and young people in community campaigns can really influence policy changes.

What do we understand meaningful participation to be? Amanda Hatton poses this question and examines how we conceptualise this. Her work with children and young people across the United Kingdom informed a practice model which she discusses in this chapter. The model involves an on-going reciprocal dialogue between children, young people and adults (p. 50). Hatton's chapter highlights the quality issue in participatory work and the importance of integrity in participatory processes.

In the final chapter in Part I, Victoria Jupp-Kina examines how adults operationalise participatory work, drawing on a research project undertaken with young people and community participation workers in Brazil. Jupp-Kina's work exposes some of the tensions and barriers in participatory work and in doing so highlights the hidden or unintended outcomes of participatory work with children and young people. When reflecting on the participatory process the impacts were found to go well beyond speaking out, as discussed in the case study of one young woman. The transformational potential of participation is once again illustrated through the articulations of young people engaged in these participatory projects.

Part II of the book looks at some examples of the spaces in which intergenerational processes of participation, representation and contri-bution can be seen. This section is introduced by Youthforia and Dan Moxon and starts by discussing the methods the group used to review two chapters, one on child language brokering in families and one on youth social capital. The group raised a set of issues in their discussions about the chapters, which related directly to their experiences of being empowered and disempowered in professional and familial exchanges including as child language brokers, and in terms of their access to or exclusion from public spaces. These valuable contributions bring insights from the lived experiences of children and young people to the research and practice issues which Siân Lucas and Paulina Billett present in their respective chapters.

DOI: 10.1057/9781137379702.0006

In Vicky Johnson's chapter we are introduced to the 'Change-scape' model, an attempt to account for the multi-dimensionality which characterises the participation of children and young people. Drawing on examples from different parts of the globe, Johnson illustrates the development and potential of both the model and the process of participation. Importantly she argues that starting with theory can alert both facilitators and children and young people to the development of participatory approaches that work in their context.

Billett's chapter examines young people's access to public space. The media representations of young people would sometimes have us believe that our public spaces are mobbed by young people; the privatisation and subsequent exclusion of young people from formerly public spaces poses serious questions about how young people are treated as citizens and as consumers. Whilst Billett discusses these issues in the context of Australia, they are relevant to other countries as well. The shift towards young people's occupation of virtual space challenges the notion that we can simply move young people on, and provides a level of privacy for young people that has hitherto been absent in their lives. Conversely, virtual spaces and young people who occupy them are subject to surveillance, scrutiny, threat and public exposure. Billett's discussion draws attention to the questions about young people's use of public space and the on-going power struggle between them and adults, and the subsequent impact on young people's social capital.

International migratory movements and globalisation expose a range of issues about childhood and children's contributions in families. Language brokering can enable access to goods and services as well as facilitate social relationships and community cohesion. The involvement of children as language brokers (CLBs) brings a set of concerns related to their maturity and capacity to translate, interpret and advocate for adults, be they a member of the child or young person's family or local community. These issues and the tensions experienced by children and young people who interpret are discussed in Lucas's chapter. CLBs opine that such brokering is a normal part of everyday life, at least for some children, and, as Lucas argues, supports cognitive and cultural development and language acquisition skills and produces certain stressors. Drawing on a qualitative study of CLBs in England, Lucas presents a case study which illustrates the range of language brokering activity 'Simran' undertakes for her family. In doing so Lucas exposes the contribution that CLBs like 'Simran' make to their immediate family and society,

DOI: 10.1057/9781137379702.0006

as well as drawing attention to the unresponsive systems which have neglected to provide effective language services.

Part III of this book considers the intergenerational practice of co-research with children and young people. This section is opened by a co-written chapter produced by Cath Larkins and a group of disabled young researchers. In this chapter the young people discuss the work of Kerawalla, Hughes and Michail, all of whom work with and write about children and young people as researchers. Larkins and the young people's group describe the process of co-authoring the chapters. They found the models discussed by Kerawalla, Hughes and Michail to be helpful and make suggestions for effective child/young person led research, which include reflecting on the processes involved to ensure that adults relinquish power – and for adult researchers it is clear that time and intensity of the work involved should not be underestimated if this process is to be meaningful for children and young people. Researcher commitment and engagement with children and young people as individuals, as well as with group participation, are key factors for the success of research which is undertaken in partnership with children and young people.

In her chapter Lucinda Kerawalla brings together issues related to civic participation, inclusion and children's rights in her discussion of a project that illustrates the processes involved in a community research project which draws on inquiry learning theory and practice. The model draws together disciplines of knowledge from education and sociology, and provides a starting point for a community-based research project which was carried out beyond the confines of the formal educational establishment. Kerawalla applies the model to the development of a research project with girls and young women (Girl Guides) and illustrates how the model facilitated the shift from them focusing on their individual opinions and views about the local community shopping facilities to achieving a group-wide consensus about what was needed in their community.

Continuing the theme of young researchers, Samia Michail discusses the shift towards this position for children in research, specifically in relation to the motivations of children and young people who lead research projects. Michail draws on developmental theories of attachment and argues for academic attention to be paid to the relationships between young people and adult researchers. The Child Led Research (CLR) discussed in this chapter was carried out by children and young people who were marginalised or excluded in some way and were receiving support from community-based services. However, the CLR project moves beyond seeking views of children and young people as service-user participants, instead facilitating their involvement as researchers and prioritising relationship-based approaches. In reflecting on the process, Michail describes how flexibility in the design of the programme was crucial to being responsive to the ways in which children and young people chose to engage (or not). Michail's work also raises the challenge of how such projects encourage children to adopt a researcher role – albeit a temporary and time limited one – and children will eventually return to their everyday lives.

The final chapter in this book is by Martin Hughes, and he reflects on how children and young people experience their engagement as co-researchers. Using Q sort methodology Hughes seeks to understand the viewpoints of young researchers. The explanation for employing Q sort in this context is grounded in it being an ethical method which gives voice to all participants. He identifies five distinct ways in which young people have experienced their engagement in research; three of these can be seen as co-researching. Hughes's study raises some important questions about the extent to which children and young people's role as researchers is congruent with the requirements of the research. Indeed Hughes suggests ownership by young researchers tends to be limited to aspects of the process rather than expecting them to engage with the whole.

The theoretical underpinning to these three final chapters combines rights, philosophy and epistemology. The glue binding these chapters together consists of the values and integrity of the researchers who wish to engage children and young people in research above and beyond the more common tokenistic consultative status they are often ascribed. In the conclusion to this edited collection, we consider how the conversations between children and adults contribute to our understanding of the three themes around which this book is focussed – participation, citizenship and intergenerational relations – as well as setting out some of the challenges which lie ahead for children, young people and adults in continuing the participatory project.

Note

1   See also http://www.dvigc.com/book/introduction/

DOI: 10.1057/9781137379702.0006

2
Children and Young People as Protagonists and Adults as Partners

Roshni K. Nuggehalli

Abstract: *Locating children and young people's research within a rights frame ensures children and young people's agency, while also challenging power relations between them and adults. The chapter discusses examples from the Concerned for Working Children's (CWC) experience of facilitating children and young people as 'research protagonists'. The role of adults as partners in enabling research is emphasised, which forms the basis for children and young people's citizenship and strengthens participatory democracy. The chapter proceeds to highlight the risks of children and young people's research losing its grounding in a rights frame through institutionalisation and 'disciplinisation' as a topic of study within the childhood studies field. Questions are raised regarding what drives adults' interest in children and young people's research and the potential implications of disciplinisation.*

Joanne Westwood, Cath Larkins, Dan Moxon, Yasmin Perry and Nigel Thomas. *Participation, Citizenship and Intergenerational Relations in Children and Young People's Lives: Children and Adults in Conversation.* Basingstoke: Palgrave Macmillan. DOI: 10.1057/9781137379702.0007.

DOI: 10.1057/9781137379702.0007

Introduction

Participation is a natural instinct for children, young people and adults. It fulfils the basic need to be part of a group and build an identity through membership and a sense of community. Children and young people have a right to express opinions and participate in decision-making that affects their lives and communities. For children and young people's meaningful and empowering participation, information is critical, both as a right and as a source of power. Locating children and young people's research within the rights frame can ensure their agency, while challenging power relations between adults and children and young people.

Proceeding from this conceptual grounding, this chapter will show how information management is of critical importance for rights-based work with marginalised children and young people. These children and young people form the primary constituency of the Concerned for Working Children (CWC), a development agency based in India. Examples from the organisation's 30-year-long experience in facilitating children and young people's research and advocacy will be discussed. Children and young people's need for research and life-altering possibilities does not always relate to their economic situation, but to their degree of social, cultural and gendered marginalisation. For these marginalised children and young people, research or 'rights-based information management' is a part of a logical sequence towards efforts at effecting change in their lives. They transform their research into advocacy for their rights with various stakeholders, including their communities and governments. This approach recasts traditional definitions of their research from children and young people as subjects or informants to children and young people as 'research protagonists'.

The primary responsibility for facilitating children and young people's research lies with adults, and the chapter reflects on the role of adults as partners in enabling information management as not only a life-skill but as a critical component of participation, forming the basis for children and young people's citizenship. The scope and context of reflexive adult engagement and responsibilities in children and young people-led research will be discussed.

The chapter will proceed to highlight the risks of children and young people's research losing its grounding in a rights frame through the process of institutionalisation and 'disciplinisation'. The emergence of

DOI: 10.1057/9781137379702.0007

research by children and young people as a new and independent topic of study within the larger and well-established childhood studies field is recent. In comparison to the institutionalisation trajectory of women's studies, childhood studies is still very much adult-led, which while being both necessary and relevant is different from the knowledge building where – as the marginalised group – children and young people themselves have a role in directing research and theory. The power relations between adult-led research on children and young people and children and young people's research arising in response to adult perspectives will be discussed. Questions will also be raised on what drives adults' interest in children and young people's research and the potential implications of disciplinisation.

Participation as a right and an ideology

CWC has been working in the area of children and young people's participation for over three decades and even prior to the United Nations Convention on the Rights of the Child (UNCRC) 1989 articulation of children's right to participate in decision-making. CWC's experience points to the importance of articulating the politics and ideological frame of the child-rights discourse. Consequently all theorising and practice undertaken by CWC has situated children's rights within the ideology of participatory democracy.

Scholars from a variety of disciplines have emphasised the participatory democracy frame as an alternative vision to liberal technocracy and runaway neoliberalism.[1] CWC strives to imbue children and young people's participation with principles of social justice, where CWC 'see[s] social hierarchy as constructed, rather than as inevitable' (Miller, 2012, n.p.), and which requires a 're-socialisation of adults and children' (Reddy and Ratna, 2002, p. 9) and the decentralised structures and processes for holding governments accountable (Gaventa, 2003). Realisation of the participatory democratic ideal entails a shift in traditional, and often entrenched, ways of governing.

Stating politics upfront and not treating 'ideology' as a negative word has ensured clarity in the direction of CWC's child-rights work. Children and young people's right to participate in decision-making and self-determine the course of their own lives is what distinguishes rights-based work from welfare interventions,[2] leading to empowering possibilities.

DOI: 10.1057/9781137379702.0007

Information as a critical element for empowering participation

To answer the question of how to enable children and young people's meaningful and empowering participation, CWC evolved a 'triangle of empowerment', with three main components (Reddy and Ratna, 2002, p. 9). First is the strength gained through democratic organisation and leadership, while another is access to and use of financial, human and material resources. A critical third component is information, both as a right and as a source of power for children and young people to influence decisions. Children and young people should not just have access to, but must be able to appropriate information towards transforming their condition.

In the context of information gathering and research, Kellett (2005a) traces the shifts in thinking and practice from children and young people being treated as 'objects' of research, to a view of children and young people as 'subjects' and 'participants'. A more recent consideration is of 'children as researchers in their own right, or "active researchers"' (p. 2), which acknowledges the importance of children and young people's voice and their role in reflecting and analysing the world from their own perspective. CWC followed a similar trajectory in the field of research, evolving processes called 'rights-based information management' or 'children and young people's research' (for purposes of this chapter), wherein children and young people themselves identify research needs, design the framework and methodology, develop and administer tools, and analyse findings. Importantly, it enables children and young people to transform their research into advocacy for their rights with various stakeholders. For instance, they have convinced their village governments to stop the illegal sale of alcohol, have influenced negative attitudes towards alcoholism (CWC, 2010) and have contributed to long-term village planning.

Grounding 'children and young people's research' in protagonism theory

While the difference between CWC's approach to research and traditional definitions that regard children and young people as merely subjects or informants is evident, we would like to emphasise another

DOI: 10.1057/9781137379702.0007

key distinction from the growing body of knowledge and work on children and young people as active researchers. The children and young people who conduct research in CWC's working areas refer to themselves as 'research protagonists'. Understanding what that means and the implications it has for the field of children and young people's research is significant.

The concept of children and young people's protagonism itself is rooted in the understanding of children and young people as the centre of their communities and societies. For a child protagonist, participation is a means to advocate on issues concerning them and transform life situations. Child protagonists view participation as a political intervention and as a right to intervene in changing their environment as active subjects. Manfred Liebel (2007) captures the development of the protagonism discourse:

> The discourse over children's protagonism draws from the popular protagonism movement that actively fought for liberation and better life conditions for excluded and exploited population groups in Latin America... As with popular protagonism, which underlies the sovereignty and creativity of these classes and people, children's protagonism increases awareness of young people's capabilities and demands their independent and influential role in society. (p. 62)

Clearly, protagonism is not just about influencing one's own life, but about playing a role in a larger environment. Liebel (2007) goes on to describe two 'dimensions' of protagonism, the first of which relates to children and young people's capacities and abilities to play an active role in their world, while the other relates to accepted norms and roles for children and young people as a part of existing social structures (p. 64). Seen in this context, protagonism pushes the boundary on children and young people having a 'voice' and being autonomous individuals, encompassing the concept of children and young people playing an active role in society and having the ability to change it according to their own ideas and perspectives.

CWC recognises children and young people's protagonism as an extension of the ideals of participatory democracy. As protagonists, children and young people contribute to building a participatory democracy, and in turn such an environment encourages and supports their protagonism. In CWC's facilitation of children and young people's protagonism, the focus is on both dimensions identified by Liebel (2007). All research

DOI: 10.1057/9781137379702.0007

undertaken by children and young people in CWC's working areas is a means and process for them to play an active role in their world. They are active researchers, yes, but they are also active change-makers. Similar to feminist researchers who challenge traditional male-centric versions of gender research, child research protagonists add original insights to the body of work on childhood and children and young people's realities. Furthermore child research protagonists challenge accepted norms of adultism and paternalism, just as feminist researchers use their research to challenge patriarchies. For these child research protagonists, research without avenues for converting it into action has little meaning.

By positioning research as a tool that enables children and young people to advocate for change, there is little scope for adults to influence the decision for children and young people to carry out research. Rather than asking the (adult-led) question whether children and young people can do research and whether they can do it well, CWC explores how we can enable children and young people to use research as a tool to make a difference in their lives. Without devaluing other forms of research, CWC's experience shows that children and young people's research rooted in protagonism theory has deep implications for empowerment and social justice. This is a critical difference between CWC's approach, examples of which are discussed in the next section, and some of the institutional and academic conceptualisations of research by children and young people in the North.

Children and young people as research protagonists: making change happen

Child-rights friendly Panchayats

During the monsoon season in Kundapura region of southern India in 2012, children's unions were involved in making their Panchayats[3] child-rights friendly. The trigger was the tragic drowning of 12 children in various villages in local ponds, holes and wells in which rain-water had collected. Children's unions in these villages identified this as an urgent problem that needed addressing and approached CWC for facilitation support.

Their first objective was to collect information on all the open water collecting holes in their villages so that they could inform the entire

DOI: 10.1057/9781137379702.0007

community, including the elected representatives of these danger zones. Additionally they wanted testimonies from adults, families and other children on their perspectives for protection of the community. They decided to use tools of resource mapping, interviews with teachers, families and children and focus group discussions to collect relevant information. During mapping they talked to adults and children recording the routes taken to work and to perform errands; areas that children played in and areas described as hazardous. Marking the results on a map they had visual proof that these ponds, holes and wells had sprung up along the way to school, home, work places and other areas that children access regularly. Children from these unions had received prior capacity building and training in research from CWC, and in a matter of a few weeks they were able to generate resource maps identifying the danger zones in all 56 Panchayats in the Kundapura sub-district.

The children developed a questionnaire that was largely graphic, so young and non-literate children could also participate. They realised that these ponds and holes were built without any information to the rest of the community or even to the elected representatives, and were extremely dangerous for children as they had no safety mechanisms. The child researchers generated a detailed set of suggestions and recommendations for barrier protection using fencing and forms of cautioning. They were surprised to learn that many of the protection measures were in fact part of the traditional culture for building open ponds and holes to collect rain-water. It was only in recent times and in the quest for quick and inexpensive infrastructure that local knowledge was being ignored and all Panchayat-level work was being outsourced to people with no understanding of local realities.

With the support of CWC, children obtained appointments with their elected leaders at the Panchayat and district level. They selected representatives among themselves to share the findings and present their recommendations at the meetings. The majority of these meetings were successful in that children's perspectives were seriously considered and acted upon. For instance, as a result of their advocacy, the district commissioner sent out a notice to all Panchayat elected representatives to make their villages child-rights friendly by ensuring fencing around the open ponds, holes, wells and ditches. Over the course of six months, Panchayat governments carried out the process of making their water bodies and other dangerous zones safe.

DOI: 10.1057/9781137379702.0007

The news of the children's research and efforts quickly spread across the villages, and many villagers, youth groups and others approached the children's unions to volunteer their time and resources in doing the fencing work. Teachers participated in awareness drives at schools and elected representatives sponsored awareness programmes throughout their electorates. Several unions also set up social monitoring systems of tying a red ribbon to a prominent tree in a village until the elected government oversaw the entire fencing work. Once complete, the children replaced the red ribbon with a white one thus holding the governments accountable.

Clearly children are deeply impacted by events in their communities, and yet they are able to carry out high-quality, multi-method research on issues relevant to their lives, arriving at alternative options with the facilitative support of adults. With adequate capacity building and support from adults, they are able to straddle personal testimony and empirical analysis, equally valuing both. Furthermore, as protagonists they can use findings to advocate for change in their lived realities in the wider community, thus establishing and proving their role as change-makers in their villages.

Adults as partners: responsibilities and ethics

In both the processes of identifying danger zones and addressing alcohol abuse, children and young researchers gained self-confidence and recognition, but also faced several challenges at the personal, family, school and community level. Adults have a strategic and critical role to play in facilitating processes of research by children and young people. Conceptualising the role of adults as partners with children and young people in their research is a useful frame of reference.

Through the protagonism lens, interactions between adults and children and young people regarding research should be respectful and mutually reinforcing.

> [A]dults should deconstruct the complex myth of research into processes that are understandable and doable by children, helping them to translate their 'desire' to use information as a tool for negotiation into a 'process' of rigour and validity from which they learn to draw their own conclusions – which may be very different from those adults might draw. (Lolichen, 2010, p. 168)

DOI: 10.1057/9781137379702.0007

Making space for children and young people to draw their own conclusions may upset traditional knowledge, adult perspectives and accepted norms. Indeed, this is an expected outcome of any participatory democratic process.

If such processes are to truly play out and input into children and young people's research, adults have a responsibility to 'change the rules of the game' in a way that children and young people's analysis and participation can move past traditional barriers and oppositions. An enabling environment based on values of democracy and critical thinking that is serious yet enjoyable is necessary. Children and young people must feel confident and safe to state their opinions and participate voluntarily. The enabling environment must also extend to the interactions children and young people have with decision-makers in their homes, schools and communities. Adults have a responsibility to facilitate children and young people to effectively interface with existing power centres and ensure that any backlash and conflict does not negatively impact the researchers. Consciously creating enough space for children and young people to move at their own pace and in their context is critical (Lolichen, 2010).

Moving beyond the considerations of confidentiality and consent alone, ethical questions must consider complexities of who controls the research design and who makes decisions on methodology, data analysis and conclusions. The answer to these questions determines whether or not children and young people's research is within the frame of participatory democracy. Along with adult facilitators, child researchers have a responsibility to reflect on who participates in the research and who is left out and the implications of these choices. The reflection must proceed to aspects of ownership of data and who decides what to update and who has access and ability to use information. Another central question is whether the process can sustain and what are the contours of sustainability?

Disciplinisation of children and young people's research?

The emergence of children and young people's research or research by children and young people as a new and independent topic of study within the larger and more established field of childhood studies is

DOI: 10.1057/9781137379702.0007

recent. A useful starting point for exploring this area is to reflect on how its parent, childhood studies became institutionalised in higher education research and training, and compare that to the course of institutionalisation and disciplinisation of women's studies. Unlike women's studies, which in most of the North arose as 'the academic response to the women's movements and the equality ideology of the 1970s' (Widerberg, 2006), childhood studies was mooted by and continues to be led by adults. Women's studies centres and departments seek to contribute to knowledge building and radical thought emanating from and influencing the women's movement. Studying children and childhoods at the higher education level by default implies that adults (men and women) are the ones thinking about children and young people, leading to a wide range of research that positions children and young people as passive objects, as subjects and sometimes as participants in action research (Kellett, 2005b). Ann Oakley (1994) captures this dilemma, '[W]e learn not about children's perspectives, but about adults concepts of childhood ... [and] much work on the concept of childhood is adultist' (p. 23).

The voices of the children and young people's movements from across the world, if included, are in the nature of participants rather than as drivers of knowledge and theory building. In spite of the value of adult perspectives in the area of children and young people's research, they do run the risk of presenting children and young people as a 'work in progress' rather than as individual and collective agents in the here and now (Oakley, 1994). In this context and as the marginalised group, children and young people's research is seen to emerge in response to adult-driven research and perspectives akin to the origins of feminist research and methodologies. As discussed in the section on protagonism theory, this approach adds great value to children and young people's articulation and analysis about their own lives, enhances adult's understanding about childhoods and is a tool for children and young people to effect change.

When this process begins to take on institutional moorings, a primary question that emerges is whether research and knowledge building by children and young people can mutually coexist and reinforce adult-led research on children and childhoods. While there is broad agreement on the benefits to children and young people of doing research, will we view them and their research as an area to be studied for generating our own insights, or will we view them as academics view feminist researchers, as a group capable of generating rigorous knowledge and critical reflection?

DOI: 10.1057/9781137379702.0007

Will we be able to value their analyses and directly incorporate that knowledge into deepening our own insights? Is it sufficient to share children and young people's knowledge base as case studies or narratives, or can we treat it on par with adult-generated knowledge? These questions do not afford easy answers and perhaps require large-scale shifts in adult thinking towards a legitimisation of knowledge generated through children and young people's research and perspectives, moving beyond merely viewing this knowledge as an improvement or value-add to childhood studies.

A related reflection is on the risks and implications of children and young people's research getting institutionalised as a 'discipline' or independent area of study. It is established that institutionalisation affects ways of doing any discipline and vice versa. How research by children and young people gets institutionalised and contoured into a discipline will depend on the ideologies and principles underpinning adults' interest in it. If we consider children and young people's research as a microcosm of a larger political ideology and theoretical exploration, then there is a strong likelihood that it will help the discipline of childhood studies move from its often adultist focus to one that is more child-centric and dialogical. If the only purpose of facilitating children and young people as researchers is to answers adults' questions about ability and to assume (often in a paternalistic manner) that children and young people must derive the benefits of engaging in research, then children and young people's research risks losing its grounding in a protagonism and rights frame. The advantages of interdisciplinary insights and linkages are also likely to be lost through this approach.

Critical questions include:

▸ What are the implications and outcomes of either a top-down or bottom-up process of institutionalisation and potential disciplinisation of children and young people's research? What are the specific implications for adults and for groups of children and young people, particularly marginalised groups?
▸ If institutionalised, how do academics and practitioners address the potential depoliticisation of children and young people's research as supported by organisations like CWC?
▸ How can the knowledge hegemony that disciplinisation often establishes be addressed and newer ways of researching and learning explored?

DOI: 10.1057/9781137379702.0007

▸ Despite the lack of a historical role for children and young people in higher education research and training, is it possible to arrive at a trajectory for institutionalisation of children and young people's research that follows a new paradigm of action research and dialogical methodologies in the true spirit of children and young people as protagonists and adults as partners?

▸ How can children and young people's research strengthen the rigour and analyses of adult-led research?

▸ How can we avoid the homogenisation of children and childhoods in the study of children and young people's research?

▸ In the area of children and young people's research, who validates knowledge generated and who become owners of knowledge and of theory?

Discussions on these should spread to outside academic circles, engaging with children and young people's movements and the adults who support them.

Conclusion

For marginalised children and young people, the close link between participation and information cannot be overstressed. Both as a process and as a tool, research is important for children and young people to express their voice and to achieve goals they set for themselves. Collecting information from and about their communities gives children and young people control over their lives. They are able to place their experiences within larger frameworks – and draw the courage and resources to find alternatives to their conditions.

These avenues for protagonism are relevant for children and young people across the world, including from the North. Marginalisation occurs on a daily basis in children and young people's lives – from school strikes that break out occasionally in different areas to the simmering angst in Egypt, Turkey and Brazil. Research and participation need not be the vestiges of controlled environments – children and young people find ways to explore and express themselves constantly. Adults have a pivotal role in supporting this expression and preventing backlash, but more importantly in helping children and young people so that they can be protagonists in their own lives.

DOI: 10.1057/9781137379702.0007

Children and young people's research opens up new possibilities for them, but it also exposes practitioners and academics to new dimensions of knowing and doing. How adults use these opportunities is determined by the politics of children and young people's agency. CWC's work points towards the benefits of participatory democracy by recognising children and young people as research protagonists and facilitating them as equal partners. Areas for reflection and practice in this area are many and if pursued have potential to contribute to strengthening children and young people's rights as well as in realising democratic ideals.

Notes

1   Including John Dewey, Riane Esler, John Gaventa and Carole Pateman among others.
2   Nandana Reddy, director development, The Concerned for Working Children, India, personal conversation.
3   Panchayat is the lowest level of administration in the system of local government in India. The term 'Panchayat' refers to both the geographical and administrative units as well as the elected body, which acts as the local council. A Panchayat is composed of a cluster of villages and several Panchayats constitute a Taluk.

DOI: 10.1057/9781137379702.0007

3

Moving from Talking to Action: Reflections on Increasing the Impact of Participation

Yasmin Perry, Cath Larkins and Preston Youth Council

▶

Abstract: *This chapter outlines the methods and approaches used to facilitate the involvement of young people in reviewing several chapters of the. The young people compared and contrasted the participatory aspects of the research discussed by Anne Crowley and made some suggestions drawing on their own experiences of being involved in participatory projects. Similarly, in their discussion of Nuggehalli, Hatton and Jupp-Kina's work, the young people reviewing the chapters distinguished the different elements and aspects of participation and the development of participatory approaches which are young person-led. In conclusion the young people reviewing these chapters suggested that a greater emphasis on comparative work would elicit a better understanding of the context of participatory projects and allow for discussions about what works.*

Joanne Westwood, Cath Larkins, Dan Moxon, Yasmin Perry and Nigel Thomas. *Participation, Citizenship and Intergenerational Relations in Children and Young People's Lives: Children and Adults in Conversation.* Basingstoke: Palgrave Macmillan. DOI: 10.1057/9781137379702.0008.

This chapter is written by Yasmin Perry, Cath Larkins and young people from Preston Youth Council. Many of the members of the council helped us in planning, organising and running the Global Conversations conference on which this book is based, but only one of them (Edward) continued to participate in writing this chapter. We therefore asked other members of the Preston Youth Council to join in reviewing and writing this chapter. In total eight youth council members participated and looked at four chapters. The chapters in this section are all about getting young people involved in decisions that affect their lives, the lives of their families, their local communities and their countries.

How did we write this chapter?

The eight members of the youth council who were present at the first meeting split into two groups. One group, which included Edward and Yasmin, looked at chapter summaries that Yasmin had written. The other group, which included a young person less confident in speaking English and peers who could act as translators, listened to a verbal summary of the chapter, given in a 'story-telling' approach by Cath.

The groups thought about:

1   What themes were identified in each chapter?
2   What was missing that relates to the topic of each chapter?
3   How all this related to the young people's lived experiences?

Their thoughts were all written down on flipchart paper and Yasmin went back to the group two weeks later to see if what was written in these notes was correct and to discuss Roshni's chapter with them. Cath then wrote up the chapter using '*quotation marks and italics*' for the words written by and from young people on the flipchart paper. This draft chapter was emailed back to the Preston Youth Council coordinator who checked with the young people that the chapter accurately reflected their views. No further changes were made to the chapter following this final review.

Key themes in young people's participation

Anne Crowley's chapter explores participation in four different types of activities in different countries. The group identified that the key

DOI: 10.1057/9781137379702.0008

theme in her chapter was 'impact'. That is, whether participation leads to change. They noted big differences between the types of activities that were described and focussed particularly on two case studies that Anne set out. They made the following contrast:

> The group in India were 'aged 6-18, called a parliament, met every week and looked at school teachers, removal of bars, the road to the village and spiders'.
>
> The 'youth forum in Wales, where 100 people meet every 2 months and is about talking to councillors' talked about the 'same sorts of things as the Preston Youth Council'.

They noted different impacts:

> In India there were positive changes, improvements were made, they had support from adults and pressure from elders in the village helped make a difference.
>
> In Wales they got skills, more confidence, but no change. If they had had longer they might have got more of a change.

The group made the following suggestions from what Anne had described, to explain why there was more impact in India.

> In India it is action, in the UK it is talking.
>
> India care more about what the YP say than in the Wales/UK example.
>
> What they are asking for in India is more achievable; children have more citizen rights to make a difference.
>
> Children are clear what they want.

The group noted important things that, as Anne had mentioned, helped change happen: *'relationships'*, *'skills'*, *'surveys'*. They also suggested that other things were important in achieving engagement and impact:

> Motivate us!
>
> Provide transport.
>
> Resistance and persistence – we have to resist when they try to ignore us and it takes time to make changes happen.
>
> Banging on about it for 3–4 years.
>
> We need opportunities to say what we want.
>
> Workers need to give choices, different timings, provide openings for us to talk to others and to be honest about what is possible.
>
> We need support – money, families, schools, councils, and the police – because what we can afford to participate in sometimes depends on costs and our incomes.

DOI: 10.1057/9781137379702.0008

Change happens because people see us everywhere – it is best for children and young people to be involved in everything then we have a greater chance of making a change somewhere.

Tell people what you are doing.

Amanda Hatton's chapter looks at why we are asking for children and young people's views, how we are asking, whether we are truly listening and how we ensure this participation is meaningful. She describes activities based around the idea of 'staying safe' and different levels and types of participation in workshops, children's event and a conference. She suggests participation should be a dialogue and that the process is meaningful because of the relationships and a focus on both the activity and achieving impact.

The young people who reviewed this chapter noted. *'Listening to what people say'* is essential. In these examples, *their participation was 'directed by what adults wanted to do this led to some political bias'*. Amanda shows the need for a focus on *'involvement'* and *'communication'* but also *'the need for feedback/follow up'*. The young people who took part in the activities Amanda describes said there was *'no feedback and follow up after the event'*.

The group contrasted the experiences described in this chapter with what they do in their youth forum, where they said they experienced good participatory practice.

> We are involved in all aspects of planning and leading workshops with adult support. There is a balance of leadership between adults and young people, depending on who is present in the group. We always feedback after events to evaluate them and we always get given feedback afterwards to say what has happened.

Although they valued Hatton's emphasis on feedback, they also suggested something might be missing from the model she put forward: 'Young people's involvement in planning/leadership is the first stage'.

Victoria Jupp-Kina's chapter looks at the gap between theory and practice in participation. She describes a series of six participatory workshops with community workers and young people in Brazil. She gives details about how the workshops were run. She explains that the people who took part in these workshops were able to experience what it was like to actually participate in different activities. Like the Preston Youth Council members themselves, these groups in Brazil included as participants young people who are facilitators in other group settings.

DOI: 10.1057/9781137379702.0008

The review group identified that there were key themes in Victoria's work. Crucially that '*understanding of participation increases with experience of participation*' but also that part of understanding comes from '*the feeling of being a participant*'. They also noted that Victoria had described how for participation to work well '*feeling safe and comfortable is really important*' and that '*[f]eeling safe and comfortable brings confidence*'.

The group agreed with Victoria that emotions are really important in participation and suggested some next steps to consider:

> How to inspire confidence in participants.
>
> How to make sure participants feel safe and comfortable.
>
> The role of different situations and environments in which participation takes place.
>
> The extent participants are from the same or different back grounds.
>
> Facilitators are also participants.

A lot of the themes in this section then echo the key points that are raised in Roshni Nuggehalli's chapter which can be seen as key points for learning about how to do participation better. One is 'young people taking the lead', taking action themselves as well as inspiring others:

> Young people actually doing things for themselves, with a slight help from/ with adults.
>
> Young people worked to spark interventions by workers to make decisions.
>
> Young people took it on themselves to do things.
>
> Young people found out why people are drinking then educated others so that there was support.

The group said participation works when it is 'based on young people's understanding' of their own lives and needs and the things they find out about through research:

> Young people know what young people's problems are.
>
> We should get more involved in research and do our own consultations.

A final key learning point identified was the 'speed' with which action was taken: 'India don't dilly dally around – they get straight to the point. But in the UK, it takes time to get to the point'. Finally, reflecting on all the chapters in this section, they felt that greater understanding of context can help explain why participation is working in some places and not in others. So they suggested there should be further comparative

DOI: 10.1057/9781137379702.0008

work that seeks to *'explain why'* there are differences between countries. Summing up their other points, this should explore the influence of environments; participants' backgrounds, confidence levels and emotions; the extent of lead taken by young people; the nature of the activities and actions followed; the timescales; and the role of feedback in achieving the changes that young people seek to achieve through their participation.

DOI: 10.1057/9781137379702.0008

4
Evaluating the Impact of Children's Participation in Public Decision-Making

Anne Crowley

▶ Abstract: *In recent years the principle of children's participation has become much more widely accepted but still, the practice remains remarkably free from empirical scrutiny. Evidence of the impact of children's public participation eludes capture and there are real challenges in disentangling the complexities of it all. This chapter explores the conceptual, methodological and practical challenges of measuring the impact of public participation. With reference to a critical review of four case studies, it argues for a renewed focus on accountability and on ensuring that children's views are listened to and taken into account, not just 'expressed'. The case studies suggest a number of factors that can work as enablers and/or inhibitors in turning, children's 'voice' into 'influence'. It can no longer be left to chance.*

Joanne Westwood, Cath Larkins, Dan Moxon, Yasmin Perry and Nigel Thomas. *Participation, Citizenship and Intergenerational Relations in Children and Young People's Lives: Children and Adults in Conversation.* Basingstoke: Palgrave Macmillan. DOI: 10.1057/9781137379702.0009.

Introduction

In recent years both internationally and within the United Kingdom there has been unprecedented attention given to engaging children and young people in decision-making around the design, provision and evaluation of public services. The drive to include children and young people as 'policy actors', as a legitimate group in the policy-making process (Arnott, 2008), has led to the burgeoning of youth and children and young people's forums and clubs operating at community, school, municipal, regional and national levels. The principle of children and young people's participation seems to be widely accepted but the practice has remained remarkably free from empirical scrutiny. For something that is held to deliver a number of benefits, we still know little of the extent to which these are actually realised.

It has been argued that because participation is a fundamental human right this is a sufficient basis upon which to assume that participation by children and young people is of benefit (Burton, 2009). However, for a number of reasons it is important to examine the impacts of children and young people's participation in decision-making. Some of these reasons are highlighted later in this chapter with reference to empirical research, but the two primary reasons are, firstly, the concerns raised by adults and children and young people alike that children and young people's participation in decision-making can be tokenistic, a tick-box exercise that fails to deliver any substantive change (Sinclair, 2004). Understandably, this perception can turn off many would-be beneficiaries who arguably have better things to do with their time. Decision-makers need to be held accountable to feeding back to children and young people on the ways in which their views have been taken into account in the design and delivery of public services. Secondly, in the new era of 'austerity' persuasive evidence about the benefits (or not) to children and young people, organisations and communities, of children and young people's participation is needed if funding and political support is to be sustained (Crowley, 2013). As Lansdown (2006, p. 24) suggests, it is important to demonstrate the efficacy of children and young people's participation if we are to get the investments in the necessary legal, social and economic supports to enable it to become a reality for children and young people.

This chapter explores some of the key conceptual, methodological and practical challenges of measuring the impacts of public participation, and

DOI: 10.1057/9781137379702.0009

with reference to recent research into the impact on policy and service development, of four different children and young people's forums, the chapter argues for more robust empirical scrutiny of the policy impact of children and young people's participation.

Background

The growth of children and young people's participation in the United Kingdom can be traced through a number of developments including pressure from young people's user groups (in particular young people in care) and the rise in the idea of the 'consumer citizen' in government policy over the last 20 years (Cockburn, 2010). However, despite attention from academics, policy-makers and practitioners and considerable investment by governments, the question of 'what difference does it make?' has received surprisingly little scrutiny. For example, the findings of a major review on service user participation in social care in the United Kingdom suggested that it was not possible to report on the effects of participation because there was little monitoring and evaluation of the difference that this type of participation was making (Carr, 2004).

This is also the case with public participation involving adults. Burton (2009, p. 263) notes the lack of empirical scrutiny into efforts to support 'more active forms of citizenship in which various decision-making processes are open to public participation' and cites a range of conceptual, theoretical and practical issues in measuring the benefits of public participation – many of which have resonance with children and young people's participation. Burton goes on to call for more work to address these issues and the development of 'more robust, relevant and reliable frameworks for evaluating the impact of participation' (p. 264) bemoaning the fact that many evaluations of the effects or benefits of citizen participation say little about the research design or the methods used to collect and analyse data.

Against this background, the research on which this chapter draws sought to evaluate the impact of children's participation in four case studies, two in Wales and two international examples (see Figure 4.1).

The chapter now turns to explore some of the conceptual and methodological challenges of evaluating children and young people's public participation, and outlines how these challenges were navigated in the research.

DOI: 10.1057/9781137379702.0009

Lamberton Youth Forum	Marlings School Council	CHIP Advisory Group	ASHA Village Forum
A local authority youth forum for young people aged 11-25 in south Wales. About 100 young people are members of the forum, representing school councils, youth clubs and other youth support services. The forum meets bi-monthly and works to influence policy and services that affect young people. Issues to be worked on are selected at the annual AGM. The issues worked on by the forum during the course of the research included: the availability and accessibility of careers advice; the allocation of Educational Maintenance Grant (EMA); improving the environment in poor communities (particularly finding better ways of dealing with litter/rubbish).	A newly established school council in a primary school in south Wales. Members are aged between 4-11 years of age. Each year group elects two members to sit on the school council for the school year. The school council meets fortnightly and works on issues of their choice, although in reality they look to the support teacher to suggest a range of options. The issues worked on by the school council during the course of the research included: a Healthy Eating campaign; toys and equipment for the playground; fundraising for the Haiti earthquake.	An advisory group of children who are beneficiaries of an international non-governmental organisation. The children's advisory group has 12 members. There are two young people from each of the six 'regions' of the world that the NGO works in. The advisory group meets annually in London and works intermittently through email during the year. The issues worked on by the group during the research included: an accountability charter; campaign against the closure of a programme in one country; establishing mechanisms to ensure that decisions taken by the board of trustees and the senior management team are informed by the views of child beneficiaries.	Neighbourhood children's Parliaments (NCPs) set up in rural villages in Tamil Nadu, south India. The villages are Dalit – the lowest caste in Indian society. All children aged between 6 and 18 years are automatically members of the village NCP. The parliament elects ministers including a prime minister, an education minister and a health minister and others as required. The NCPs meet weekly and are supported by older young people who also provide support with education in an after school club. The issues worked on by the NCP during the research include: the removal of an of an illegal liquor store in the village; replacing an approach road; and the quality of teaching in school.

FIGURE 4.1   *Case studies*

DOI: 10.1057/9781137379702.0009

Conceptual and methodological challenges

There are a number of difficulties with any attempt to measure public participation or even democracy – its extent, its durability, its comparative standing and its impact (Beetham, 1994). It is important to be aware of these if reasonable foundations are to be laid for trying to measure impact and improve our understanding of public participation. As Burton (2009, p. 264) argues, the conceptual facets of public participation need to be addressed because 'without a reasonable degree of conceptual clarity ... any subsequent practical measures would be built on shaky foundations'. Highlighted here are a few of the related conceptual challenges arising from the research and descriptions of how these were addressed.

Defining public participation

Participation is an ill-defined concept with understandings ranging from 'taking part' to full-blown citizenship (Thomas, 2007). There is also a distinction between participation in collective or public decision-making and participation in decisions about the lives of individual children and young people. The research on which this chapter draws was concerned with children and young people's collective participation in decision-making about public policies that affect children and young people's lives, particularly children and young people's involvement in the planning, implementation and evaluation of public services and in the governance of social welfare and development organisations.

Kirby with Bryson (2002) notes there are different levels and types of involvement in this public decision-making including one-off consultations (e.g., surveys, focus groups); regular or extended programmes of involvement at both the organisational (e.g., school councils) and area-wide strategic levels (e.g., council youth forum; social action youth groups); as well as integrated daily participatory approaches (e.g., democratic schooling). Projects vary from consultations through to self-advocacy projects with differentiation related to project aims and the relative power between children and young people and adults (Lansdown, 2006).

The literature makes a distinction between 'formal', managed, top-down participation and more 'bottom up' participative democracy

DOI: 10.1057/9781137379702.0009

(Cockburn, 2010; Badham, 2004). Thus youth forums, school councils and national, government-funded consultations would be examples of the former, and young people's mobilisation to protest against the Iraq War in March 2003 an example of the latter (Badham, 2004).

Cantwell's (2011) argument that sometimes we try and obtain too much from the United Nations Convention on the Rights of the Child (UNCRC) at the expense of securing everything possible on the basis of its actual requirements is persuasive. He argues that inflating children and young people's participation rights as set out in the CRC waters down the accountability aspects of *human* rights (his emphasis). Addressing the challenges of defining participation are thus perhaps best dealt with by reverting to the more legalistic definition contained in Article 12 of the UNCRC and expanded upon in the Committee's General Comment (Committee on the Rights of the Child, 2009) as it applies to children and young people collectively participating in the governance of public services. This incorporates the right of children and young people to be heard, to be listened to and for their views to be given due weight in all matters affecting them.

Lundy (2007) also suggests that a focus on these constituent parts of Article 12 of the CRC can be help us to constructively move away from the 'cosiness' of terms such as 'the voice of the child'. Lundy's concepts of children and young people's right to 'audience' and to 'influence' in addition to 'space' and 'voice' provide a useful analytic tool to help develop understanding of the factors that work to either enable or inhibit children and young people's forums to impact on policy-making.

Conceptualising and measuring the impact of children and young people's participation

Kirby et al. (2004) provide a useful framework for understanding the changes that result from children and young people's public participation. This framework spans three broad dimensions of change: the impact on children and young people themselves in terms of confidence, skills and access to opportunities; the impact on social and power relations between children and young people and adults; and finally, the impact on policies and services. Indicators of change related to each of the dimensions were adapted as illustrated in the following section. The research focused primarily on the third dimension of change, that is, the impact of children and young people's participation on the policies and services they were seeking to change.

DOI: 10.1057/9781137379702.0009

Children and young people's participation: core dimensions of change

1 Impact on children's personal development and well-being
   ‣ Children's self-esteem and self-confidence increase
   ‣ Children acquire additional skills
   ‣ Additional measures are selected by children
2 Impact on social and power relations
   ‣ Improved structures and/or resources and for involving children in decision-making and governance
   ‣ Children report improvements in:
      ‣ adults' awareness of children's rights
      ‣ being listened to by adults
      ‣ feeling respected by adults
   ‣ Children report that they can change things – influencing the services and community provision that affect them
   ‣ Workers in relevant service agencies report:
      ‣ higher levels of awareness of children's rights belief
      ‣ expectation in children having a say in decisions about public services
   ‣ Additional measures are selected by children
3 Impact on policies and services
   ‣ Changes in the policy or service (the changes the children want to see).
   ‣ Children or young people report that they receive good enough feedback on how their views were taken into account and what difference they made
   ‣ Service providers report increased awareness of the issues raised by children and young people (issues to be specified)

Evaluating the influence of children and young people's involvement in any policy or service development process is complex. Policy-makers and service planners will often have to balance a variety of interests and discerning the relationship between evidence and policy-making is notoriously problematic (Nutley and Webb, 2000; Tisdall and Davies, 2004). The literature reveals different views on the operation of the policy-making (and practice development) processes and most importantly very different definitions of what constitutes legitimate and 'valid' evidence on which to base public policy. Understanding the competing research

DOI: 10.1057/9781137379702.0009

ideologies and the consequential value placed on the contribution of service user knowledge and experience to the development of evidence-based policy and practice (e.g., are the experiences and opinions of service user perceived as 'valid' evidence) is key to understanding how service users' participation in policy debates may or may not impact on policy and public services (Beresford, 2007).

Leaders of the normative evidence-based movement in social care (Sheldon, 2001; Macdonald, 1996) emphasise a broadly rational, linear relationship between research and policy but this conception of the policy-making process has been critiqued for being over-simplistic (Webb, 2001). Policy-makers, it is argued, are not necessarily rational actors and human rationality is bounded. We need to recognise the complexities of the processes and the importance of power and status differences (Shaw and Shaw, 1997). Different approaches are thus needed to understanding and valuing 'evidence' such as those that utilise diverse sources of knowledge rather than single, method approaches. The challenge is how best to design processes that can synthesise and integrate evidence of different types to inform policy decision-making.

The question of what counts as valid knowledge and evidence is thus key in determining how to conduct an investigation into the impact of children and young people's participation on policy-making. Participatory approaches thus need to place value and legitimacy on children and young people's own accounts, in line with a standpoint that views children and young people as social actors in their own right. This knowledge (and that gained from practitioners and the policy-makers the children and young people tried to influence) can then be used to inform broader judgements about the difference that children and young people and young people's involvement has made to policies and services. The research design and the methodology selected are discussed in the next section.

Research design

The research was designed to enable the changes in policy and public services that the children and young people in the forums said they wanted to see (their 'change objectives') at point A, to be contrasted with

DOI: 10.1057/9781137379702.0009

stakeholders' accounts of what changes had been brought about by the children and young people's influencing activities, 9–12 months later, at point B. Points A and B were determined by the annual cycles of the forums, for example, at Marlings (the school council in south Wales), at the beginning and end of the school year. It was recognised that there will be a multitude of variables that could intervene and impact on policy outcomes between points A and B. Nonetheless, this design allowed for a sense of appraisal of two points in time that allowed for some inference about the content and nature of the impact of the children and young people's forums on policy-making. Mid-point reviews afforded valuable opportunities to observe the forums and the interactions between the support workers and the children and young people and gather their reflections on the influencing activities the children and young people were engaged in.

The primary data collection methods selected were semi-structured interviews with adults, focus groups with children and young people, observations of each of the forums in action and analysis of official documents relating to each of the forums. Focus groups and interviews were conducted with the participating children and young people and the support workers at both the 'before' and 'after' stages, that is, *before* the children and young people began to try and influence the policy-making process and then again *after* their 'participation' or involvement had concluded. Semi-structured interviews were conducted with senior managers and sponsors of the forum, that is, elected members in Lambertons, the local authority youth forum in south Wales, the chair of the school governing body in Marlings school) and the local councillor in India over the course of the study period and (in the 'after' stage) with policy-makers or service planners who were the subject of the children and young people's influencing activities (the 'decision-makers'). Fieldwork visits to the case study sites were also undertaken at a mid-way point to gain data on progress from both the children and young people and the support workers and to observe the forums. Detailed field notes were taken of these events and analysed alongside the participants' accounts. Documents, including the minutes of the forum meetings over the study period, policy statements and annual and other evaluative reports on the forums were also analysed. The longitudinal nature of the data collection arrangements is illustrated in the following section.

DOI: 10.1057/9781137379702.0009

Data collection methods

Before	During	After
▶ Focus groups with children and young people ▶ Observation of forums ▶ Semi-structured interviews with support worker(s)	▶ Observation of forums ▶ Documentary analysis: minutes of meetings; reports on activities; policy documents ▶ Focus groups with children and young people and support workers (to gather reflections on progress) ▶ Semi-structured interviews with senior managers and sponsors	▶ Focus groups with children and young people ▶ Observation of forums ▶ Semi-structured interviews with support worker(s) ▶ Semi-structured interviews with those people the children and young people were trying to influence (e.g., service planners, policy-makers) ▶ Documentary analysis

A number of analytical tools were used to help interpret the data including Kirby et al.'s (2004) core dimensions of change; Lundy's (2007) concept of 'voice' and 'influence'; Treseder's (1997) wheel of the different degrees of participation; Cornwall's (2004) concepts of participation 'spaces'; and a set of recognised practice standards (Save the Children, 2007). A policy network analytic framework was employed to explore linkages between the different actors and interest groups and consider concepts of resource exchange and bargaining (Tisdall and Davies, 2004). The analysis also explored examples in each of the four case studies of how control was exerted from the top and influenced the 'what' and 'how' of policy-making and children and young people's participation therein. A reflexive, iterative and systematic approach to data analysis was employed with triangulation as a key strategy for enhancing the validity of the research.

The chapter now considers selective findings of the research before concluding with some final comments on the need for a more positive and constructive approach to monitoring and evaluation of the impact of children and young people's participation in policy-making.

Findings

When comparing what the children and young people in Wales set out to achieve by way of influence (e.g., in Lamberton the youth forum

DOI: 10.1057/9781137379702.0009

wanted to see a more flexible, drop-in careers advice and information services) with the situation 12 months later, it was hard to discern any resultant changes in policy or practice. This is not to say that the forums' activities did not have any impact. The impact on children and young people themselves of their 'participation' in the representative structures of the youth forum and the school council in terms of confidence boosting, skills development and horizon widening was frequently reported and observed. It is also important to consider that the impacts of the children and young people's participation on policies and services might become evident outside the time-frame of the study, that is, after 12 months. Influencing policy from the outside takes time with policy change most likely to take place during short-lived 'policy windows' producing the best opportunities for policy change (Kingdom, 1984).

In contrast, in India, the National Children's Parliaments (NCPs) had a discernible impact on a number of priority issues of concern they had brought to the attention of the local council and relevant district-level government departments. Issues taken up by the NCPs include:

▶ The need for an approach road to the village
▶ Elimination of an illicit liquor shop
▶ Cleaning of overhead water tank
▶ Accessing resources for a Balwadi[1] centre
▶ Upgrading of a primary school
▶ Destruction of an insect nest

In all these cases positive changes or improvements were achieved. Of particular interest here is that the NCPs are encouraged by the adults who support them to work on issues they have a chance of affecting and to target local decision-making processes. The children and young people and community leaders interviewed all praised the achievements of the NCPs. In one case (the destruction of the insect nest), one of the village elders reported that they had put pressure on the local council to sort out the insect nest to no avail but action was taken by the municipality as soon as the children and young people protested and wrote a letter.

This comparison of the outcomes of children and young people's participation in public decision-making as presented here is crude and requires much more sophisticated discussion of the different

DOI: 10.1057/9781137379702.0009

contexts, the varying power dynamics and the functioning of the participatory structures in each of the four case studies, but a number of themes emerged as to factors that work as 'enablers' and 'inhibitors' in children and young people achieving change in public decision-making.

First and foremost, children and young people's voice is much more likely to have an influence when they are seen as rights holders and not as 'trainee' citizens, where they are supported and enabled to have effective audiences with the people who can make the changes they want to see. There was evidence from the Wales case studies that children and young people's participation in the forums was viewed primarily by senior managers, forum sponsors and support workers as a space for citizenship training. While the equivalent people in India also saw the NCPs as an opportunity for children and young people to learn and exercise responsibility, the primary objective for the NCPs as expressed was much more about children and young people being rights holders and the NCPs working to help them to improve their situation in the here and now.

The work of James and Prout (1997), Mayall (2000) and Jenks (2005) highlights the importance of how children and young people are perceived and conceptualised. If children and young people are seen as 'little-people-in-the-making' who need opportunities to 'practice' participation in order to become good future citizens, then the processes of children and young people's involvement and the impact on the participants as young adults is of more interest than the impact of the children and young people's engagement on public services. If, however, children and young people are viewed as social actors with their own perspectives and abilities to influence decision-making as children and young people, and as rights holders who can call to account those who have a corresponding duty to fulfill that right, then the impact on the actual decisions being made about public services is seen as more important (Qvortrup, 2003).

Other enabling factors suggested from the analysis included: being clear about the objectives of the participation; being focused on well-understood policy or practice opportunities; integration between child participation structures and similar structures targeting other civil society groups at a local level. The importance of policy networks and the linking of the children and young people's resources with other influencing factors emphasises the important role of supporting adults in

DOI: 10.1057/9781137379702.0009

reflexively navigating the tensions that Shier (2010) identifies in children and young people's public participation.

Conclusion

Evidence of the impact of children and young people's public participation remains difficult to capture and there are real challenges. For example, disentangling the complexity of the 'intervention' and the different cultural meanings associated with civic participation. Nonetheless, the research suggests that the reasons for the lack of research into the outcomes of children and young people's public participation (e.g., youth forums and school councils) may not just be because of methodological challenges, but also because no impact or immediate outcome was ever really conceived by the sponsors, the objectives are primarily about the *process* of participating and of children and young people learning to become good future citizens rather than exercising their rights now, as children and young people.

But the routine monitoring and evaluation of the impact of children and young people's participation is now increasingly important. A focus on impacts or the outcomes of children and young people's participation as well as the quality of the process helps to clarify who are the duty bearers and their responsibilities and also assists children and young people in gaining a greater understanding of what they hope to achieve and what support and resources are needed to strengthen child participation. It can also provide evidence to support the case for political commitment to the realisation of children and young people's participation rights and encourages funders to see the benefits of investment in strategies to promote child participation. If we cannot articulate or evidence the outcomes of children's participation in these times of financial austerity, there is a real risk to the sustainability of the new institutional structures for children and young people's participation – certainly in the United Kingdom.

More needs to be done to emphasise the accountability adults have to not only enabling and supporting children and young people to express their views but also to ensuring that those views 'are taken into account', in line with Article 12 of the UNCRC.

It is hoped that the approach to evaluating the impact of children and young people's participation and dealing with some of the conceptual

DOI: 10.1057/9781137379702.0009

and methodological challenges set out in this chapter provides a stimulus for further developing robust and appropriate methods for evaluating the impact and outcomes of children and young people's participation in public decision-making or policy-making.

Note

1   Pre-school nursery.

DOI: 10.1057/9781137379702.0009

5

Shallow Democracy: In Other People's Shoes – Listening to the Voices of Children and Young People

Amanda Hatton

▶

Abstract: *This chapter focuses on how adults listen to the voices of children and young people and engage in a dialogue to create meaningful participation that is accessible and inclusive, rather than tokenistic. Complexities of participation are explored, examining different levels of engagement with young people involved in a consultation process with a Safeguarding Children's Board, where they had the opportunity to express their views as part of a collaborative process with adults.*

Joanne Westwood, Cath Larkins, Dan Moxon, Yasmin Perry and Nigel Thomas. *Participation, Citizenship and Intergenerational Relations in Children and Young People's Lives: Children and Adults in Conversation.* Basingstoke: Palgrave Macmillan. DOI: 10.1057/9781137379702.0010.

Introduction

This chapter is about how adults listen to the voices of children and young people. As a practitioner and researcher I am interested in this because participation with children and young people may not always be conducted in a way that is meaningful to them as individuals, their lives or circumstances, or to the issues that concern them. Elaborate participation or consultation events may be good at asking children what they think but then, often, even with the best intentions, nothing really comes of what they have said. In this way the process may be regarded as tokenistic. Meaningful participation should be accessible and inclusive, a dialogue which involves both listening to the voices of children and young people and responding constructively to them.

This chapter will explore some of the complexities of participation, examining different levels of engagement with children and young people, and will put forward a model to help address these issues and challenges. This study considers when we ask to hear their voices: why are we asking; how are we asking; but most importantly are we truly listening, and how do we ensure that this is meaningful and not tokenistic.

The aim is to offer a practical model of participative practice, based on children and young people's views, drawing on findings from my own research of a consultation process, 'Bounce', delivered by Derbyshire's Safeguarding Children Board. The main focus of consultation was located within the discourse of rights, highlighted through the United Nations Convention on the Rights of the Child (UNCRC), 'The Children Act 1989', the local safeguarding children agenda and the national Every Child Matters (2003) agenda, translated into legislation in 'The Children Act 2004'. The consultation was around the outcome and theme of 'Stay Safe', one of the five outcomes from the national 'Every Child Matters' initiative, which is 'staying safe: being protected from harm and neglect' (DfES, *Every Child Matters*, 2003, p. 6). The process used a range of arts and media to consult creatively with children and young people on the following five 'staying safe' sub-themes:

▸ Safe from maltreatment, neglect, violence and sexual exploitation
▸ Safe from accidental injury and death
▸ Safe from bullying and discrimination
▸ Safe from crime and anti-social behaviour in and out of school
▸ Have security, stability and are cared for (DfES, Every Child Matters, 2003)

DOI: 10.1057/9781137379702.0010

The project was a countywide initiative, involving over 200 children and young people, and consisted of three stages, including workshops in five secondary schools, a 'staying safe' children's event and a 'staying safe' conference with both multi-agency practitioners and young people from the schools. The workshops in the schools fed into both the children's event and the adult conference. The Staying Safe children's event provided a day of creative workshops to stimulate discussion with the young people from the schools and other children, and raise awareness about staying safe and what that means to young people. At the Staying Safe adult conference the young people from the schools presented their workshops and ideas, posed their questions about staying safe and led the practitioners to respond using the same creative art forms. Artists worked with the young people in the secondary schools to support them in using the creative art form to develop their ideas to create a workshop around their stay safe theme, with content that both reflected their views and would enable them to gain the views of other children and young people at the children's event and of practitioners at the conference. The creative art forms used were hip-hop, animation, drama, sculpture and creative art installation.

Method

My initial focus was to look at how effective this project was as a meaningful process and the impact of using creative arts and media. I developed this to focus on the wider theme of participation, to include the concept of voice and, more importantly, listening. I gathered data using a range of methods including participant observation, photographs, questionnaires and semi-structured interviews, involving the children and young people in collecting and generating the data. Using participatory research methods enabled the children and young people to be engaged in the process on their own terms, within their own frame of reference, particularly using media from their own popular culture. I used participant observation throughout each stage of the project which allowed me to observe the interactions between the children and young people and the adults in creating the data and art forms and also the dialogue that followed when the children and young people presented their views and perspectives to the adults.

DOI: 10.1057/9781137379702.0010

Background

This research critically engages with recent debates and concepts surrounding participatory practices and methods. Theoretical interpretations of this project were based on Hart's (1997) model of participation, considering different levels of engagement and choice for children and young people in events organised by adults. The study looked at the difficulties of events often being organised by adults concerned with giving children a voice and research that may be promoted as being participatory whilst children and young people's voices are restricted. Tokenism may occur through the need for organisations to include participation to secure funding, or unintentionally as a result of practitioners not fully understanding the issues. The study looked at how participation may be tokenistic but how in this project, there could be choice and opportunity for children and young people to be involved in varying degrees in projects and events with adults. The study also demonstrates what Kirby et al. (2003) described as a degree of participation and through the involvement of children and young people at different stages of the project links to 'pockets of participation' (Franks, 2011, p. 4), where value in their participation was developed by having ownership of different aspects.

Consideration was given to the agendas of participation, highlighted through the following statement: 'Many participation initiatives start from adult priorities rather than those of children and young people. It is clear that, given powerful adult agendas at play, "having a say" is insufficient to achieve effective and meaningful participation for young people' (Clark and Percy-Smith, 2006, p. 2). This concept specifically linked to my research focuses on how participation can be a meaningful process and I linked this to participation using creative arts and media. Using creative arts and media demonstrates the importance of the collaborative process through physical engagement with an activity and participating in a more interactive way can make the process more meaningful (Christensen and Prout, 2005; Cook and Hess, 2007; Hill, 2006; Thomas, 2007).

Analysis of this study recognises participation as a process of social learning, reflection and dialogue between children and young people and adults (Percy-Smith, 2006). This concept of participation links to the project through the shared conference with the children and young people and the adults and also links to the concept of 'communicative

DOI: 10.1057/9781137379702.0010

action spaces' (p. 169) where the power relationships were negotiated, evidenced by the young people leading the workshops at the adult conference.

Findings

Understanding different levels of participation

This study demonstrates different levels of participation (Kirby et al., 2003) where the young people had the opportunity to express their views, and although the project was based on an adult agenda, their views were listened to and taken into account. Throughout the project there were different levels of participation including workshops in schools, the children's event and then leading the workshops at the adult conference.

The children and young people were more actively involved, and had more agency, in the workshops in the schools, enabling them to get into a more thoughtful space, learn the skills and subsequently to think about the safeguarding theme, working collaboratively with the artists, creating 'pockets of participation' (Franks, 2011, p. 4). At the children's event, young people leading the workshops was central to them truly being active participants. In leading the workshops at the adult conference the young people also felt that the adults were listening to what they had to say about being safe. Participation as a process of social learning, reflection and dialogue (Percy-Smith, 2006) between children and young people and professionals can be seen in how their presence enhanced the delegates' engagement and debate, highlighted by one of the artists: 'The participants really valued the opportunity to engage with a group of well-motivated, positive young people who had prepared the topic they were exploring and had a wealth of opinions, ideas and experience to share' (cited in Hatton, 2010, p. 152).

Being involved in these 'communicative action spaces' (Percy-Smith, 2006, p. 169), where the power relationships were negotiated, was evidenced with the young people leading the workshops at the adult conference. A practitioner commented: 'Involving young people in conversation with adult practitioners was very effective and should be expanded, their opinions were valued' (cited in Hatton, 2010, p. 155). This session provided a space to listen to the young people and reflect on the learning from these communications. A key feature of this was

DOI: 10.1057/9781137379702.0010

the reciprocity in the dialogue and exchange. What emerged was that the process was most meaningful because of the relationships, shown through the enjoyment of the young people and adults working together, having discussions and a dialogue.

This process clearly gave the young people opportunity to participate at a different level to their usual experience and provided opportunity to participate by developing different identities according to the different environments (James and Prout, 1990). The comments of the young people highlighted that they enjoyed working with the artists, hearing the views of other young people and being listened to by adults. This suggests that the important factor of their participation was the opportunity for dialogue and discussion.

Critical analysis demonstrates that when considering participation as a process it can become more complex in understanding that at different times throughout the stages of a project there may be different levels of participation. This therefore can be challenging when trying to implement participation as policy.

In the workshops at the adult conference the adults were led by the young people and worked collaboratively with them to respond to issues about staying safe. This challenged the perceptions of adults but also the perceptions of the young people as the adults genuinely listened to them, as one of the young people observed: '[W]hen you started talking they were actually listening and asking more about it' (cited in Hatton, 2010, p. 152). The implications for practice show that by involving all parties in a genuine dialogue both adults and children and young people can develop a better understanding of the issues as well as the perspectives of others. By holding a conference for both children and young people and adults, spaces outside the usual more controlled environments developed more opportunities to participate.

Model of participative practice

As outlined earlier, there are a range of theoretical discussions on models of participation. One of the limitations of interpreting or understanding participation only in terms of consultation, expressing views or giving voice is that this is only one part of the process of participation.

As part of the study, a focus group with children and young people, aged 14–19, provided their views on the barriers that prevented their

DOI: 10.1057/9781137379702.0010

active participation. Their responses highlighted that on occasion they felt stereotyped, not listened to and that their opinions were not valued. There was pressure to say what the adults wanted and they also highlighted that they were fed up with different people asking the same questions.

From an analysis of this study, I put forward a model of participative practice that could help to address these issues and challenges and support meaningful participation (Figure 5.1). This model is based on dialogue and the following key stages of the process:

▸ Communicate
▸ Listen
▸ Respond

Communicate

A range of methods that enable young people to participate on their own terms should be used. The use of creative arts and media was a central focus that created an experiential learning process that engaged with the art forms to respond to the themes and create a dialogue in a more interactive way. Using these creative media enabled the young people to respond because 'these issues came in from the side, not driving it, because it took

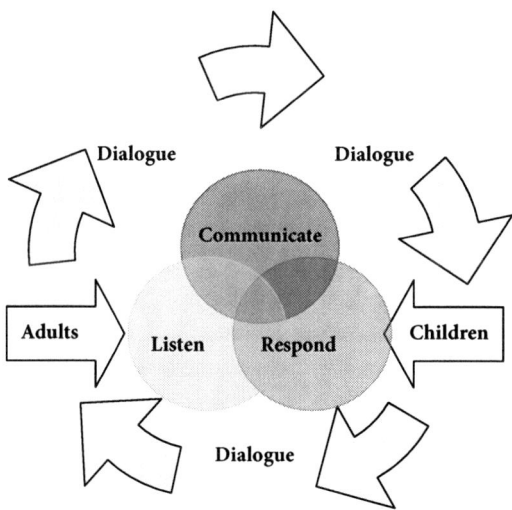

FIGURE 5.1 *Hatton's model of participative practice*

DOI: 10.1057/9781137379702.0010

the young people into a different thought space, shaping it in their own time when they were ready' (cited in Hatton, 2010, p. 143). Therefore, we understand that this was a collaborative process through physical engagement with an activity (Cook and Hess, 2007) and that being involved in the process is just as important as the outcomes (Thomas, 2007). Used collaboratively, engaging in an activity can bridge communication between children's inner and outer worlds but also between children and adults.

As Hill (2006) recognises, many one-off events focus on enjoyment as part of the process, and this was one of the key features for the children and young people involved in this project. Using creative methods positioned the adults differently, through power dynamics of the children and young people being the experts in the methods, relating to their own frames of reference (Christensen and Prout, 2005). A wider range of methods and approaches enabled children and young people to communicate their views but also provided a collaborative way of working that engaged the adults in more informal dialogues with them, rather than being seen as authority figures.

It is important that adults show a genuine interest and do not stereotype children and young people as a homogeneous group. There should be an awareness of ways of communicating with children and young people that indicate a genuine relationship and interest in their views. One of the main themes that emerged was about the quality of the relationships with workers and that children and young people can quickly spot a genuine concern to hear their views but equally a tokenistic approach, as explicitly identified by the following comment: 'A lot of the workers look like they are listening to you when you want an answer to something but nothing gets done about it so people tend not to ask anything again' (cited in Hatton, 2010, p. 193). This demonstrates that to engage with children and young people in a meaningful way, practitioners should be aware of ways of communicating and the importance of genuineness (Thomas, 2001).

Another key recommendation is that communication is seen as a process not just a means to achieving a prescribed set of outcomes (Thomas, 2007). It is important that this be a process of dialogue, reflection and interpretation (Clark and Moss, 2001) that is undertaken collaboratively in an appropriate way and in an appropriate environment.

Communication should be a collaborative process and a space that provides opportunity for a genuine dialogue that enables shared understanding, social learning and communicating meaning together.

DOI: 10.1057/9781137379702.0010

Regarding the use of language in the communication process the focus group recommended that adults abandon their professional discourse, particularly the jargon, which can act as a barrier to open communication. Adults should engage with young people on their terms, using language that is accessible and does not support any inequality of power that may exist (Bearne and Marsh, 2007; Greene and Hill, 2005; Prout, 2002).

Listen

The focus group felt strongly that professionals should listen to them, not only using active listening skills but paying attention to what they have to say about their own lives and about other issues as well. Rather than the issues being determined by adults, the process should facilitate children and young people to be listened to about issues that impact on their lives, about their priorities (Boylan and Dalrymple, 2009). Practitioners should also communicate with children and young people in a way that recognises them as experts in their own lives (Clark and Moss, 2001). Rather than seeing listening as one stage, it should be seen as part of a process, a two-way process that involves listening and being listened to (Thomas, 2007). The theme of the value of being listened to emerged from the views of the children and young people when they felt they were not truly listened to.

In addition they highlighted that as well as not being listened to, what they said was not acted upon, and this made their participation pointless. The main recommendation is that listening to the voices of children and young people should be embedded into everyday practice to develop a listening culture. To really listen to young people is to empower them by hearing what they say.

This model is put forward as a model of participative practice and when compared with the Lundy (2007, p. 936) model, which conceptualises Article 12 of the UNCRC, it is important to highlight the responsibilities and legal implications 'that children have a right to have their views listened to (not just heard) by those involved in the decision making processes'.

Respond

Finally the key feature to this model is to respond, whether that is through action or dialogue, but by being honest about how their views will be used, if anything can or cannot be done, but importantly to tell

DOI: 10.1057/9781137379702.0010

them what will happen next and why their views have been sought. There should be a shared understanding of the process as a whole, how will the views that the children and young people have communicated be responded to? The importance of dialogue and communication should be recognised through the feedback and sharing of information. There should be a shared and agreed response on how to address the issues raised. The focus group expressed how they felt that the process of participation can sometimes be meaningless and have no value:

▸ Doesn't matter what you say nothing changes
▸ It all goes in just another file
▸ We never hear back
▸ Even though we are asked our opinions and we ask for something it never happens and they never get back to you about it. (Cited in Hatton, 2010, pp. 192–193)

For participation to be a meaningful process, these comments highlight that they want to know what has been done with what they say, or if indeed something *can* be done. If nothing can be done then, the adults should be honest and at least let them know the outcomes.

This model builds on the theoretical models and works of Hart (1997), Kirby et al. (2003), Percy-Smith, (2006) and Franks (2011) and could be used at any level, throughout all the parts of a project, allowing for different partners in the process to lead and take responsibility at different times. In using this model, expressions of voice and communication need to be interpreted thoughtfully and critically as part of an ongoing dialogue.

Conclusion

In summary, this model recognises that relationships are key to enhancing participation and that each stage of this model to communicate, listen and respond are an essential part of a shared experience within a negotiated space that acknowledges the agency of children and young people and their capacity to participate. In this process of communication and dialogue, it is important that we listen respectfully and act upon or respond to what children and young people tell us and be honest about how we will use this information. A final recommendation in using this model is to address embedded practices of power and authority, the way we listen to, interpret and act upon what children and young people say

DOI: 10.1057/9781137379702.0010

and to be aware of them through each stage of this model to develop a genuine underlying structure of dialogue.

This model focuses on the relationship within the dialogue and the affective dimension of creative and participatory work, through each stage of communicating, listening and responding, considering how the process feels; how it is experienced on a personal level for the individual and how this is communicated and shared. This is crucial to develop effective future participatory work that involves young people in the process, promotes understanding and brings about positive outcomes.

Key implications

Whilst many professionals have very genuine intentions to make participation meaningful for children and young people, they themselves may be constrained by the discourses and systems within which they are situated.

Consulting and engaging with children and young people takes time and resources, but in practice we need to consider how to do it well and really engage with and listen to children and young people. The ways of working and the methods for involvement can enable children and young people to become involved. There should be support to enable them to develop their own sense of agency, to resolve problems and make changes, and to increase their confidence and self-esteem. There should be value in the process of taking part, with personal benefits rather than a focus on outcomes, with a two-way communication process of listening and being listened to (Thomas, 2007).

Participation has the potential to bring groups and generations together to listen to one another, exchange ideas and negotiate a shared response. From this study I conclude that we could use this model as a starting point for any research, consultation, participation, or work in consideration of the above points, to improve relationships between young people and adults to increase the success of participation.

As a consequence of putting forward this model of participative practice, and the process of dialogue between children and young people and adults, with the three key elements being to communicate, listen and respond, I would like to ask other children and young people their recommendations for workers and researchers to do these better.

DOI: 10.1057/9781137379702.0010

6

Making the Invisible Visible: Using Participatory Action Research as a Means to Uncover Hidden Barriers in Children and Young People's Participation

Victoria Jupp-Kina

Abstract: *This chapter explores challenges when facilitating participatory processes drawing on a Participatory Action Research project with community development practitioners in São Paulo, Brazil. Using participatory methods, the workshops facilitated a participatory evaluation and team planning exercise for strengthening children and young people's participation as well as exploring institutional challenges. This chapter discusses the unexpected outcomes of this process, including understandings of participation and its personal nature and how these work to allow hidden issues of power and emotions to become more visible.*

Joanne Westwood, Cath Larkins, Dan Moxon, Yasmin Perry and Nigel Thomas. *Participation, Citizenship and Intergenerational Relations in Children and Young People's Lives: Children and Adults in Conversation.* Basingstoke: Palgrave Macmillan. DOI: 10.1057/9781137379702.0011.

DOI: 10.1057/9781137379702.0011

> I think first, above everything, it's really understanding ... For all that we ... for example I've read about it [but] when it comes to doing it there's a hole, there's a gap, there's a space, a long distance between what you understand and when you do it. Fernando, nucleus coordinator[1]

Introduction

This chapter came about as a result of some research that aimed to understand the difficulties and challenges that adults face in trying to work 'participatorily' with children and young people. As Fernando, one of the staff members who took part in the research, highlights in the epigraph there is a 'gap' between knowing something and being able to actually do it. This research wanted to understand more about the gap and work out potential ways of helping the people facilitating children and young people's participation – who are often adults – work more effectively. Although a lot has been written about children and young people's participation, the focus has tended to remain on the different participatory methods that we can use with the implication that the right method will ensure that we are being 'participatory'. However this is too simplistic as it ignores the relationship between the person or people *facilitating* the participatory process and the people who are *participating in* the process. The aim of this research was therefore to reflect on and discuss children and young people's participation with practitioners and with young people to gain an insight into this relationship and understand some of the challenges that practitioners face in transforming participatory principles into practice.

Chapter outline

This chapter focuses on one aspect of a Participatory Action Research (PAR) project with community development practitioners and young people in an NGO (non-governmental organisation) in São Paulo, Brazil. As part of the research I ran a series of workshops with the staff team, including young people employed as 'youth mediators'. The workshops were held over a period of one year and used participatory methods to discuss children and young people's participation. As a result of adopting a participatory approach to discuss participation a number

DOI: 10.1057/9781137379702.0011

of unexpected outcomes emerged from the process: namely, that it was through a combination of increasing the *knowledge of participation* with the *experience of participating* in a participatory process that some of the invisible institutional and individual barriers to effective participatory practice were revealed. This chapter will provide some examples of these unexpected outcomes and will begin to explore the implications of this experience for developing more effective and sustainable participatory practices with children and young people.

Background

The recognition of a gap between theory and practice in children and young people's participation is not new. The existence of 'huge gaps…between our learning and our behaviour or practice' (Roper and Pettit, 2002, p. 263) is a key difficulty that has become a focus of discussion and numerous books, manuals and guides have been written to try to address the gap between the theory and the reality of 'doing' participation (see, e.g., Fajerman and Treseder, 1997; Lansdown, 2001; Chambers, 2002; Driskell, 2002; Hart et al., 2004; Save the Children, 2005; Tisdall et al., 2009; Percy-Smith and Thomas, 2010). However despite this attention the difficulty in transforming theory into practice continues. More recent debates highlight that one reason for this may be because participation is a dialogical and relational process in which participants and facilitators need to be viewed as interdependent actors (Percy-Smith, 2006; Mannion, 2010). Rather than participation being a process that is about 'them' – the participants – it is now increasingly viewed as a collaborative process about 'us' – which includes *both* the participants and the facilitators. As highlighted by Mannion (2010, p. 338) this new conceptualisation of participation means that participants and facilitators are 'embodied, spatially located performers of fluid subject positions, rather than independent rational agents with immobile positions'. However this view has revealed the complexity of participation, as if we are all spatially located performers of fluid subject positions then participation is a deeply emotional process for all involved, including those facilitating the processes. It is this complexity that this research aimed to explore by working alongside both adults and young people and jointly reflecting on the challenges that 'doing' participation poses.

DOI: 10.1057/9781137379702.0011

The research: a participatory workshop series to explore children and young people's participation

The workshop series was designed to provide a space for group reflection on current participatory work being undertaken and to plan for future work. The workshop series consisted of six participatory workshops and used a variety of participatory methods designed to encourage reflection (Figure 6.1). This approach was designed to provide a safe space within which all partici-

Workshop Title	Workshop Aim	Method Used
Workshop 1: Where are we at?	General evaluation of current level of children and young people's participation	Participatory ranking of current level of children and young people's participation within project. Small group discussions to justify score given.
Workshop 2: No, really where are we at?	Focused evaluation of children and young people's participation	Variation on the 'carousel' active learning method (Chambers, 2002, p. 148). Six 'stations' with key questions to facilitate discussion.
Workshop 3: Addressing tricky issues	Discussion of power as an institutional barrier	Two methods used: reflective 'Pot of Power' tool and an adapted version of the Chapati/Venn diagramming tool (see Archer and Cottingham, 1996) using circles to reflect on levels of influence within the project.
Workshop 4: Exploring what's possible	Developing new ways of working through reflecting on the responsibility of participation	Interactive drama to enact and then re-enact a lived experience of a group member in order to reflect on responsibility.
Workshop 5: How can we get to where we want to be?	Planning for the implementation of children and young people's participation	Creation of an organisational 'menu of participation' to plan for future priorities for developing and sustaining children and young people's participation.
Workshop 6: But how do we do it?	Developing a participatory toolkit for practice	Used a participatory methods booklet developed as part of the research as an activity resource for participants to practice facilitating their own participatory process.

FIGURE 6.1   *Participatory workshop series*

DOI: 10.1057/9781137379702.0011

pants, whether members of the management committee or young people working as youth mediators, would feel free to express their views.

The unexpected outcomes of a participatory process: the impact of understanding and experiencing participation

What was so interesting about this workshop series was that it gradually became clear that it had had an extremely personal impact on some of the participants. A number of 'unexpected outcomes' emerged during final reflective interviews conducted at the end of the research process with both practitioners and young people. Ironically, it appeared that the experience of participating in a participatory process had helped individuals involved to identify and reflect on their own barriers to working 'participatorily' and to identify the collective barriers within the team and organisation. These appeared to be as a result of two things: firstly, through increasing the knowledge and understanding of what participation is and what it can involve; secondly, through providing the opportunity for people to experience participation for themselves.

The impact of understanding what participation is and what it involves

Due to limited space, I have selected a couple of examples of the unexpected outcomes. The first of these is the impact of the research process reported by one of the youth mediators. Susana was one of the older 'young people' working at the organisation; however she was also one of the shyer members of the younger staff. When asked during her final reflective interview if her understanding of participation had changed during the research, Susana replied:

> Yes. Because my thinking with regards to participation was completely different. For me, participation was only when a person spoke or how [hesitates] but with these workshops I realised that participation goes much further than speaking, but translated into written words, gestures and even symbols.[2]

What emerged as the interview progressed was that Susana related this change in understanding to a change in the way she communicated with

DOI: 10.1057/9781137379702.0011

people. When asked if the research had had an impact upon her work, Susana responded: 'I'll participate my way now, I'll write, keep sending people what I'm writing, until I completely develop [have enough confidence] to speak in public'.³ This appears to be an important point. Susana highlights that by having a clearer understanding of the various forms of participation – that it went beyond just speaking – she was able to adopt alternative strategies and participate in 'her way'. Indeed, Susana chose to participate in 'her way' during the research process by writing an open letter to members of staff to express her frustration at certain events that had occurred. Susana had never previously expressed her views in this form and I had not made any requests for any form of written feedback nor explicitly stated writing as an alternative option. What this seems to indicate is that the workshop series had improved Susana's understanding of what participation is and as a result Susana had been able to take control of *her own* participation.

Another example of the importance of understanding participation emerged as a result of the third workshop exploring institutional barriers. This workshop highlighted the need to understand the complexity of participation through the use of circles to represent and facilitate an analysis of power. When comparing the diagrams produced by the team of educators and the youth mediators a clear difference emerged between the view the educators had of their role within the organisation and the view held by the youth mediators. The diagrams highlighted that while the educators made only two connections to represent their flow of influence within the organisation – one internal via their nucleus coordinator and one external via the children and young people with whom they work – the young people connected the circle representing the educators to well over half of the people and groups of people external to the project, as well as connecting them to other people and groups internally. This highlights not only the complex nature of power but also the need to extend our understanding to include *perceptions* of power. While the educators had reported throughout the research process that they often felt quite powerless within the organisation, the way in which they were perceived by the young people did not reflect this. The young people perceived them as powerful and, consequently, held them responsible for bringing about a change. Lukes (2005, p. 66) argues that '[t]he powerful are those whom we judge or can hold to be responsible for significant outcomes'; however, this activity seemed to indicate that this is a complex process, as people's views on responsibility may

DOI: 10.1057/9781137379702.0011

not correspond. Given that transparency and trust between participants and facilitators have been identified as key features of participation, this workshop highlighted how the differing perceptions of power could be an important invisible barrier to the development of effective and sustainable participatory practices.

The impact of experiencing participation to deepen and extend understanding

While the workshop series appeared to help increase understanding of participation, it was not only this that seemed to create the personal impact for participants. According to the final reflections and feed-back from staff and young people at the project, it was the experience of participating in a participatory process that resulted in the deeply personal nature of some of the outcomes. A clear example of the impact of experiencing participation was in the final reflections of João on the second workshop that used the 'carousel' method to aid discussion. João, a nucleus coordinator at the project, felt that this method made him reflect on the importance of hearing other people and allowing this to deepen his own thinking. In other words, he began to see the relational nature of the participatory process; that it is not just about giving the space for the other person to speak, but it is about listening to what the other person has to say, absorbing that and allowing your own thinking to 'mature' as a result:

> for me this was what was really strong when you divided the whole group of [name of project] in groups and everyone could say, talk a little about participation and when you did this rotation. When I passed through each of these points [stations], my thinking was maturing. It was constructing itself in a different way because it brought questions that I hadn't stopped to think about yet. What stayed really strongly with me about the purpose of the research was to be able to look at ourselves, to be able to see these questions.[4]

What João is highlighting is that the experience of participating in the workshops provided an opportunity for him to develop 'new forms of knowledge and ways of knowing' (Kesby, 2005, p. 2042). This is an aspect that was also highlighted by one of the youth mediators, Thiago, in his final reflective interview. He describes a process of personal 'unblock-ing' whereby he overcame a previous lack of confidence to express his

DOI: 10.1057/9781137379702.0011

opinion. When asked whether his opinion about participation had changed during the research, Thiago responded:

> I felt blocked before. I think that I wasn't able to express all that I thought and I said [to myself] 'ah, you'll talk crap, why say anything? Keep quiet because I'll get more [out of it] and learn more just from listening'. But no, I understood that it's through speaking that we learn, that it's through participating that we learn, isn't it? And it's this that I'm trying to do today.[5]

What Thiago appears to be indicating is that he felt blocked 'before', meaning before he participated in the research. When asked what he felt had been positive about the research, Thiago responded:

THIAGO: I think it was good because I started to have ideas that I could use not just in the library but for me, for my own knowledge. I think it helped me a lot.

VICTORIA: How did it help you? Outside of your work?

THIAGO: That's it. In my studies. My bedroom is my study, I stay there studying, researching something and participation helps me in a way not … there won't be anyone to participate with, but participating with myself. I don't know if you're able to understand, but I think it helped me a little with this thing of being able to express what I feel. Before I didn't express myself, after the first workshop that we had with you I started to have a few more ideas, having participated. I felt part of the team. I think it helped me a lot.[6]

Thiago highlights a key point, in that his experience of participating in the workshops not only created new knowledge but that this knowledge extended beyond the space of the workshop and helped him to participate 'with himself'. In other words, he too had begun to become active in *his own* participation. In the same way Susana had been able to take control of her own participation as a result of understanding what participation could involve, Thiago indicates that as a result of experiencing participation he was able to become active in his own participation not just in the specific workshop space but within his own life.

The impact of both understanding and experiencing participation: making the invisible visible?

These examples provide an indication of the potential impact of participatory processes. As noted by Mannion (2010, p. 339) the effects

DOI: 10.1057/9781137379702.0011

of participation can be felt in 'contexts and times beyond the immediate realm of the participatory work itself'. While the objective of the workshop series had been to reflect on current and future participatory work with children and young people, the use of participatory methods within the workshops provided spaces within which the participants could critically reflect upon their own experiences and assess their own subjectivities. Through using participation to discuss participation a space was created in which participants were able to become more aware of the space and context within which children and young people's participation was to be 'performed' and to adjust their own subject positions accordingly. In essence it appears that this approach allowed for the staff team to develop a 'situated consciousness of [their] location and interests' (Kesby, 2005, p. 2046) that extended far beyond the workshop space.

The impact of the combination of increased understanding with the experiencing of participation was neatly captured by Fabio, a nucleus coordinator, in his final reflective interview. He felt that the use of a participatory approach to discuss children and young people's participation had created an opportunity for self-reflection. For Fabio, he felt that this resulted in participants beginning to connect their own inconsistencies and the inconsistencies of other people with the development of children and young people's participation:

> Many were extremely interested, not just a professional interest but a personal one as well, in relation to life, with what I think has to be, how my own life has to be. And others were uncomfortable, uncomfortable in the same meaning that it has to do with you, with the institution, with life and all that. They're the things that you can't see, can't feel, but that mess with you a lot...the research had this influence that I see as a positive. I don't know, I don't think it'll resolve the problem but it gave a transparency, a few things appeared in a few people, in a few groups that made other people understand better what is actually real.[7]

It is this aspect of transparency that seems to raise some interesting questions about how to address the gap between knowing about participation and actually 'doing' it. Firstly, it highlights the need for 'safe spaces' for reflection and discussion that allow for the invisible interpersonal and organisational barriers to participation to become visible. Secondly, it highlights the need for these spaces to be over a period of time, thereby allowing people's understanding of participation and their relationship to participation to evolve over time. Thirdly,

DOI: 10.1057/9781137379702.0011

the research also raises an interesting question about the potential role of Participatory Action Research in improving participatory practices. In this particular research process, the workshop series appeared to be one way to create the 'safe spaces' for individual and institutional reflection. In final interviews participants highlighted that it was my role as an 'outsider' that enabled me to create a space in which they felt able to discuss sensitive issues like power and reveal barriers that might have otherwise remained hidden. While there may be a series of ethical issues that this raises, it does bring up the question of how action researchers could play a significant role in helping practitioners to create these spaces for discussion and move towards addressing the theory/practice gap. After all, as effectively summarised by Paulo, the director of the project examined in this chapter: 'And I think it's a question that when people experience it they tend to believe in it, then it will grow by itself and you can change things'.[8]

Notes

1 Original Portuguese: *Eu acho que primeiro, acima de tudo, é o entendimento mesmo. Por mais que a gente ... por exemplo eu li a respeito [mas] na hora de executar tem um buraco, tem um vão, tem um espaço, uma distância muito longa entre o que se entende e na hora de fazer.*

2 Original Portuguese: *Sim. Porque o meu pensamento a respeito de participação era completamente diferente. Para mim, participação só era quando uma pessoa falava ou como [hesitates] mas com essas oficinas percebi que participação vai muito além do que falar, mas traduzida em palavras escritas, gestos e até mesmo símbolos.*

3 Original Portuguese: *Eu vou participar do meu jeito agora. Eu vou escrever, ficar mandando para as pessoas o que estou escrevendo, até me desenvolver totalmente para falar em público.*

4 Original Portuguese: *'para mim ficou muito forte quando você dividiu o grupo da [name of project] toda em grupos e todos puderam dizer, falar um pouco sobre a participação e quando você faz esse rodízio. Quando eu passei por cada um desses pontos, o meu pensamento foi maturando. Ele foi se construindo de uma outra maneira porque foi trazendo questões que eu não havia parado para pensar ainda. O que fica muito forte para mim do propósito da pesquisa foi de poder olhar para gente mesmo, poder se enxergar nessas questões.*

5 Original Portuguese: *'Eu me sentia bloqueado antes. Eu acho que não conseguia expressar tudo que eu pensava e falava 'ai, você vai falar besteira, por que eu vou falar? Deixa eu ficar calado porque ganho mais e aprendo mais ouvindo mesmo'.*

DOI: 10.1057/9781137379702.0011

Mas não, entendi que é falando que a gente aprende mesmo, que é participando que a gente aprende, né? E é isso que eu estou tentando fazer até hoje.'

6   Original Portuguese:

THIAGO: *Acho que foi bom porque comecei a ter umas ideias que pude usar não só na biblioteca, mas para mim, para os meus próprios conhecimentos. Eu acho que me ajudou bastante.*

VICTORIA: *Como ajudou você? Fora do seu trabalho?*

THIAGO: *Isso. Nos meus estudos. O meu quarto é a minha biblioteca, fico lá estudando, pesquisando alguma coisa e a participação me ajuda de uma forma não... Não vai ter ninguém para participar junto, mas participando comigo mesmo. Não sei se você consegue entender, mas acho que me ajuda um pouco esse negócio de poder expressar o que eu sinto. Antes eu não me expressava, depois da primeira oficina que a gente teve com você comecei a ter um pouquinho mais de ideias, tenho participado. Eu acho parte de uma equipe. Eu acho que me ajudou bastante.*

7   Original Portuguese: *Muitos extremamente interessados, interesse não só profissional mas também pessoal assim, em relação com a vida, com o que acha que tem que ser, como a própria vida tem que ser. E outras incomodadas, incomodadas no mesmo sentido que tem a ver consigo, com a instituição, com a vida e tudo mais. São as coisas que não dá para ver, não dá para sentir, mas que mexeu bastante... na pesquisa teve essa influência que eu vejo como positiva. Sei lá, não acho que vai resolver o problema mas deu uma, transpareceu, apareceu algumas coisas de algumas pessoas, de alguns grupos que fazem as outras pessoas entenderem melhor o que é real mesmo.*

8   This participant is a native English speaker and therefore this interview was conducted in English.

DOI: 10.1057/9781137379702.0011

7
Regional Youth Forum Conversations between Young People and Adults: The Space for Dialogue

Dan Moxon

▶

Abstract: *This chapter was co-produced by young people and an adult participation worker. Young people from Youthforia Youth Forum were supported to analyse and discuss chapters of three other authors, whose own work focussed on the space for participation and intergenerational dialogue and features in this book. Using Lucas's work on child language brokering, Johnson's work on the Change-scape and Billet's work on public space, this chapter draws out young people's ideas of power and its connection to dialogue and relationships with adults. It concludes with questions raised by the young people. Does the United Nations Convention on the Rights of the Child's (UNCRC) Article 12 go far enough for successful participation? Do adults listen to children and young people and then act, rather just listen and take into account.*

Joanne Westwood, Cath Larkins, Dan Moxon, Yasmin Perry and Nigel Thomas. *Participation, Citizenship and Intergenerational Relations in Children and Young People's Lives: Children and Adults in Conversation.* Basingstoke: Palgrave Macmillan. DOI: 10.1057/9781137379702.0012.

This chapter was written by Dan Moxon, an adult participation worker, and Abbie Rainey, Benjamin Vaughan, Callum Woodworth, Chris Mells, Elisha Stephens, Elizabeth Murphy, Emily Kay, Harry Campbell, India Taylor, Jack Anthony, Jack Whelan, Jonnie Buckingham, Kaisha Fletcher, Laraib Taylor, Leon Gledhill, Lucy Wood, Lydia Wolstenholme, Maciek Chybowski, Mollie McGowan, Nathan McPoland, Pat Farrell, Pheobe Gibson, Rebecca Brunskill, Rhianna Williams, Robyn Dooley, Thomas Scott, Thomas Taylor and Yasmina Lee. These are all young people aged 11–19 years from Youthforia, a regional youth forum in the North West of England (www.youthforia.org.uk).

To write the chapter:

1   Chapters in this section of the book were summarised on paper by Dan.
2   The summaries and full chapters were given to the group, and a group discussion was held based on these. Throughout this we talked about the group's views of different parts of the chapters, and how they fitted in with their own experiences. This discussion was audio recorded.
3   At a later date, a second discussion was held on the key themes that came out from the first discussion. This was also audio recorded.
4   The group's size was large, and the group did not always agree, so supporting them to put pen to paper to voice this chapter directly was not practical. Instead, this chapter was voiced by Dan as a summary of the discussions, based on the audio recordings. Direct quotes were used whenever possible but speakers were not named, as it was not always possible to identify which young person was speaking from the recording.
5   A draft of the chapter was emailed to the group for final comment and approval.

What does dialogue with adults mean to young people, and how does it affect their ability to participate in decisions about their lives? These are some of the questions that the authors in this section seek to answer. However, when discussing the responses the young people involved in Youthforia quickly raised a widening spiral of further issues and questions.

In her chapter on child language brokering (CLB), Lucas explores what happens to a young person when they are providing language support for non-English speaking family members to enable them to

DOI: 10.1057/9781137379702.0012

talk with other adults. The young people from Youthforia were interested in understanding the way CLB changes the dialogue young people have with the adults and the effect this has on a child. Lucas's descriptions of Simran, a child language broker, caused great debate amongst the young people, particularly when trying to agree whether CLB was an acceptable situation for Simran to be in. Like the author, the group was interested in the impact CLB has on Simran's life, and if CLB is a situation which should be avoided. Also like the author, and in contrast to conventional social work wisdom, they approached this question with no preconceptions that CLB should be avoided. Instead they sought only to understand the situation from Simran's perspective. Many questions were raised by the group such as: did relying on Simran prevent her mother from improving her own English? Did it make her unwilling, or even unable, to learn? Similarly, the group were concerned that having to provide CLB might interfere with Simran's education. The more Simran's experience was discussed the more complexities the group identified, all underpinned by questions about the effect of the dialogue Simran had with the adults around her, and the unusual family power dynamics created by this. One young man summarised some of the challenges that Lucas's chapter presents by asking: 'Who is being more limited here, the mother or the daughter?'

Ultimately the group did not agree if CLB is an acceptable situation for Simran; the young people who themselves identified as child language brokers felt that it was not a negative experience, and went on to highlight how close Simran's experiences were to their own. However many of the young people from outside of a CLB situation felt it was taking advantage of Simran, and the state and her father should do more to prevent CLB. What was clear was that all of the young people recognised that when something such as CLB alters a young person's experience of dialogue with adults, it alters their experiences of power dynamics between adults and young people as well.

When the group considered Billett's discussion on young people's exclusion from public space, the members talked about the two contrasting dialogues they had with adults when entering the public spaces. On the one hand, adults talked to them as young people at risk, in need of protection especially after the sun goes down. On the other, the dialogue with adults told them about the threat young people created in public space. Both were said to be key to young people's relationship with public space.

DOI: 10.1057/9781137379702.0012

> [T]here's like this fear [from adults] that as soon as it gets dark everywhere is suddenly filled with rapists and murderers and druggies and things like that ... [so you can't go out].
>
> Young man

> [Y]eah and older people have that fear of young people too.
>
> Young woman

Other members of the group also highlighted the problems in reducing the discussion to generalisations of 'young people' and 'adults', and how dialogues with different adults change.

> [T]o parents and others close we are the victims, but to older people and others we are the threat.
>
> Young man

Rather than just being coerced out of public space by adults, the group said they were choosing to leave public space due to the perceived threat of 'other' young people. This was a perception they acquired from their dialogue with adults. If one of the narratives from adults is 'young people are threatening', young people themselves begin to feel threatened by other young people.

> [T]here's also like stereotypes ... you would probably see police around the place where there's a lot of young people, and I wouldn't like to go somewhere where a lot of young people my age are, me myself, I would assume bad things would happen.
>
> Young man

The discussion the group had about both of these chapters highlights the way in which dialogue with adults has a complex relationship to both empowering and disempowering young people. Billet's chapter demonstrates the way in which adults' constructed narratives with young people can shape and control their behaviour, whilst Lucas's chapter shows how the power dynamic between adults and young people is challenged when modes of communication are unconventional.

For the second session the link between power and dialogue was discussed directly by the group. They were asked about the situations in which adults had power over their lives, and how this was shown through their dialogue with them. One of the first ways they highlighted was adults' power to refuse or end dialogue with them.

> When you are discussing the issue and you have one point and the adult has theirs, I tend to find the adult gives up and doesn't talk. That's a way of showing you that I'm right and you're wrong.
>
> Young woman

DOI: 10.1057/9781137379702.0012

The young people described the frustration they felt when an adult listened to them, but then ended the conversation and went on to make a decision about a young person's life themselves. This ranged from examples of staying out late, to choosing classes at school, or going to the prom. This form of decision-making was contrasted with examples when adults had taken part in dialogue with young people with the aim of reaching an agreement about a decision

> [I]f there's a decision involving me, my mum will come and talk to me about it, and I'll put forward my opinion. If mum has a different decision we just talk about it until we agree. It does depend on what the thing is, if my mum feels strongly about it, she will just bypass me.

Young man

To the young people there was an important difference between *adults listening and taking young people's opinions into account* and *adults discussing and reaching agreement with young people*. The second option was seen to be the form of dialogue that was most empowering, and enabled the young people's agency and participation the most. However, the same adult would use different methods at different times and was thus able to control the mode of dialogue.

Johnson's chapter in this section helps us develop a more sophisticated understanding of the way communication and dialogue occurs in participation, and highlights the importance of moving beyond listening to young people to explore and understand dialogue as a process for change. Johnson's Change-scape model allows us to understand more deeply the communication and collaboration that occurs between adults and young people that enables change. Equally, by considering the context of children and young people's lives and their individual identities Johnson also resolves some of the problem's raised by the Youthforia group of considering young people and adults as a homogenous group. In this way the Change-scape presents an exciting opportunity to look at existing participatory processes with a fresh lens, and consider if and how we can move beyond listening to focus on dialogue and change.

Sadly, in all of our discussions the group's experience of dialogue with adults was usually based around the adult retaining the power and making decisions on their behalf. There were many examples where adults had listened to them, but it was discussion and agreement they craved. As a result of the UNCRC, adults concerned with youth participation often talk about the importance of *listening to young people* and this defines a

DOI: 10.1057/9781137379702.0012

mode of dialogue with young people. Whilst this is certainly progression from *not* listening, listening alone may not be enough. It may be that to truly empower young people, adults need to go further, making a commitment to discuss and reach agreement with young people, rather than just take their views into account.

DOI: 10.1057/9781137379702.0012

8

Youth Social Capital, Place and Space

Paulina Billett

Abstract: *Public space plays an important role in the fostering of social capital by providing young people with places in which to come together and network. Yet the visibility of young people in public space has a long history of public concern, which has resulted in attempts, usually through legal means, to 'normalise' young people's behaviour. This has led to the restriction of what young people are able to do, the ways in which they network and the places in which this can be done, which is not only highly objectionable but also problematic. This chapter examines the meaning and transformation of public/ private space and its impact on young people's ability to foster and reproduce social capital.*

Joanne Westwood, Cath Larkins, Dan Moxon, Yasmin Perry and Nigel Thomas. *Participation, Citizenship and Intergenerational Relations in Children and Young People's Lives: Children and Adults in Conversation.* Basingstoke: Palgrave Macmillan. DOI: 10.1057/9781137379702.0013.

Introduction

This chapter discusses the struggle over public space and its impact on youth social capital.[1] Its aim is to show that place and space are not neutral concepts, but are instead sites of struggle due to their hierarchical ordering and control. The hierarchy existent in the occupation of public space has led to the alienation of young people, limiting their opportunities to come together and create social capital. I begin this chapter by discussing why young people are viewed as undesirables in public space, followed by an examination of the impact of this exclusion on their ability to come together and create social capital. Finally the chapter overviews some of the ways in which we may be able to address young people's lack of space.

The struggle for public space

Adults have always perceived young people as problematic and as challenging the social order. Parents complain about the 'waywardness' of the new generation. This perception has been strongly played out in the struggle for public space.

The struggle for the use of space can be traced to recent times. In much of the western world, the latter part of the 19th century saw a number of economic and social changes. In Australia the division of labour and urbanisation brought on by the capitalist economies saw young people displaced from the workplace by the labour laws and educational reforms (White, 1990). This change to the workplace 'gave' young people time for 'leisure', which was often spent in street corners and other public venues 'hanging out' which was seen as problematic and threatening by adults.

Yet, for most young people, public space plays an important role providing a place where they can 'hang out' and be 'seen to be seen'. Hanging out involves the negotiation of public space (Nair et al., 2002 and 2003), and social activities such as talking, eating and play-fighting (Morrill et al., 2005) but also involves the open enactment of 'risky' subcultural behaviour such as graffiti, drinking, smoking and drug use. These behaviours are perceived as threats to the moral order and threaten to subsume space intended for consumption for less desirable purposes (James et al., 1998; Matthews and Limb, 1999; Billett, 2011 and

DOI: 10.1057/9781137379702.0013

2012). Hence, when young people make a claim for space it is often met with antagonism and suspicion by the larger community, and has led to a multitude of responses by government and non-government agencies to diffuse rising tensions – usually by controlling young people's movement or 'moving them on'.

In much of the western world, control of young people in public space has been achieved through legal avenues. In Australia, there have been two main laws passed which have affected young people; the 'move on' powers, established in 1998, which allow police to move on 'nuisance' individuals; and later the Summary Offences and Control of Weapons Acts Amendment Bill (passed in 2009), whereby young people can be 'moved on' and even strip-searched if they are considered to be 'public offenders' (Farrell, 2009). In the United Kingdom the Crime and Disorder Act, also passed in 1998, introduced the Anti-Social Behaviour Orders allowing for any person over the age of ten to be fined or detained for 'anti-social behaviour'. Not surprisingly young people, and in particular those most marginalised and vulnerable, find themselves the most likely target of these initiatives (Walsh and Taylor, 2007; Farrell, 2009; Stephenson et al., 2011).

Similarly, virtual space, just like physical space, is becoming increasingly constructed through the allowance and prohibition of certain actions. However, unlike physical space, attempts to control virtual space by adults have been ineffective at best. Not surprisingly, calls for increasing surveillance of children and young people's behaviour on the virtual world are abundant, with the internet being hailed as a wedge for the 'normal' social functioning of young people (Mythil et al., 2008; Subrahmanyam et al., 2001) and thus their presence in this space is becoming largely undesirable.

For young people attempts by adults to 'normalise' their behaviour restrict what they are able to do, the ways in which they network and the places in which this can be done are highly objectionable and problematic. Surveillance of young people's attitudes and behaviours (particularly subcultural behaviour) in public space results in their actions being classified as risky, anti-social and delinquent; behaviours which must be controlled in order to keep young people and 'the future' safe (Wyn and White, 1997). The surveillance and negative connotations attached by adults to youth behaviour have led to young people reporting feelings of general mistrust by the community and experiencing an acute awareness of negative feelings directed toward them by adults (Morrow, 2001).

DOI: 10.1057/9781137379702.0013

Feelings of mistrust can lead to the withdrawal of young people into their peer groups as a kind of protective mechanism culminating in their being perceived as anti-social, disengaged and social capital deficient.

The meaning of place and space

At the same time that history shaped young people in public space as problematic, our understanding of the concepts of place and space has helped to form these views. As discussed previously, space and place are not neutral but are highly loaded terms. Place and space may mean different things to different people – think, for example, a typical location such as a shopping centre. It is a place where people work, shop and congregate; it simultaneously allows a multiplicity of meanings and experiences (consider, e.g., its meaning for a worker as opposed to a group of school friends hanging out after school). It is within this multiplicity that the source of the conflict between young people and adults arises.

The reason for this conflict is in our lack of understanding of what place and space actually mean. While masked in the common sense of language, the actual meaning of place and space is often misunderstood. A 'place' is often used as a term to describe a 'space', but the meaning of 'space' is not necessarily the same as a 'place'. Place and space are fundamentally different and at the same time co-dependent. Place in its truest sense is 'a meaningful location' (Creswell, 2004); it is based on our 'sense of place' (feelings of belonging, acceptance and sense of ownership among others). It is the *subjective* and *emotional* attachment to a physical or material location. Place also constitutes the location and locale (the actual *physical* or *material* location such as a house, a street, a park or a shopping centre) which people make use of to produce and consume meaning (Agnew, 1987). Space on the other hand is more abstract. It often denotes emptiness and volume simultaneously – for example, an empty room or a vacant block. Spaces only become places when they are vested with meaning – the empty room becomes a bedroom and a vacant block becomes a home. In short, space is place devoid of value or meaning which becomes 'place' only when endowed with value (Tuan, 1997). It is only when we give space meaning and become attached to it in some way (e.g., 'our skate park', my 'group's' benches) that space becomes place.

Yet the meaning of space and its occupation is not neutral but instead it is a heavily contested arena. Occupation of space is constructed through

DOI: 10.1057/9781137379702.0013

a number of processes which can lead to polarisation and the creation of unequal access to sectors (Lefebvre, 1991; Bridge and Watson, 2000). An interesting way to look at the occupation and contestation of space is through the work of Henri Lefebvre (1991). For Lefebvre, space is not neutral or inert, but rather, it is an ongoing production which 'subsumes things produced, and encompasses their interrelationships'. In his work, Lefebvre deals with space as an expression of the process of production, what he calls 'social space'. Lefebvre posits that space is the conduit between production and consumption by permitting certain actions, while suggesting or prohibiting others (Lefebvre, 1991). Lefebvre's thesis on social space is of particular importance when examining the use of space and place by young people, as it allows us to understand the causes of unequal access to certain spaces.

Thus, deciding who belongs and who does not belong to a particular space is an important way in which our towns, cities and world are divided and private and public spaces created (Malone, 1999). In terms of young people, this can be highly problematic. The need to maintain large sections of social space for the purpose of production and consumption means that those unable to engage in these practices are deemed 'undesirable' and are often met with hostility and resistance when they attempt to occupy these contested spaces. For young people, their exclusion from important public spaces such as the shopping centre affects their ability to create their own places to hang out, limiting their opportunities to network and to create social capital.

The effects of young people's exclusion from public space on their social capital

As we have seen, adequate spaces in which to hang out are of extreme importance for young people, as their ability to come together and prove their 'coolness' and 'social worth' is an essential part of the social capital puzzle. As I have discussed in the previous sections, a place is more than just a space as it is vested with particular meaning. Spaces which have specific meaning for young people are called 'youth specific' spaces (Venkatesh and Kassimir, 2007, p. 232). Not surprisingly, the majority of youth social capital is created within these spaces and the relationships formed during this time together are of extreme importance and for many young people 'constitutes the centre of their universe' (Morrill et al., 2005, p, 100).

DOI: 10.1057/9781137379702.0013

However, young people are restricted in the spaces in which they can gather due to economic situation and age. Unlike adults, who are able to access private spaces in which to congregate, most young people lack the age and economic resources to own or rent private property meaning that the majority must rely on the availability of 'age appropriate venues' to meet. This often requires young people to travel to meet with friends which can be difficult, as they often find themselves unable to access reliable transport. This in turn leads to young people feeling isolated, bored and disengaged from their local communities.

The lack of access to youth spaces has led to young people lamenting their lack of opportunities to have fun (e.g., see Travlou, 2003; Dee, 2008; Billett, 2011). Young people often report using streets, parks and other such spaces as places in which to congregate, though many feel that these spaces can at times be unsafe. The lack of safe public spaces in which to congregate has thrust young people into public/private spaces, such as shopping centres. These areas while being perceived as 'safer' than hanging out in the street are problematic in themselves as their use as meeting places are highly contested.

As described previously, very few locations remain true public spaces in any real sense, for the majority are either public spaces which are managed by specific organisations, such as local parks and reserves, or are private spaces with public access, such as cinemas and shopping centres (Hatzopoulos and Clancey, 2007). These spaces are increasingly based around high visibility and consumption of goods. If we cast our attention back to Lefebvre's examination of public space, we can see that public space exists as a conduit between production and consumption. As such, there is an expectation that those who frequent these spaces will do so as consumers rather than as spectators. These expectations have meant an increased regularisation and surveillance of behaviour in many of these locales in order to avert any behaviour which may threaten to modify its purpose.

Shopping centres are particular telling examples of the role public access plays within the production/consumption dynamic and its effects on young people's ability to gather and create social capital. Shopping centres are seen as exciting places to hang out by young people (White, 1995). However young people's presence in shopping centres is seldom welcome except as consumers and their behaviour is often seen as a threat to the hegemony of adult ownership (Matthews and Limb, 1999) and consumption of goods. According to White (1995, p. 36), for young

DOI: 10.1057/9781137379702.0013

people 'the shopping centre is a site for socializing first and consumption second', 'places to be seen' rather than places to shop and as such their behaviour, which is often highly visible, is perceived as problematic. The perceived threat posed by young people, together with their lack of economic power, has led to them being seen as 'undesirable' within this private/public environment, culminating in an increase in overt surveillance in the form of cameras and private security staff. The repercussion this exclusion has had is that young people are left feeling marginalised, harassed and resentful as they fail to understand why their presence is so objectionable (see White, 1990; Dee, 2008; Billett, 2011).

The need to control young people has meant that they are increasingly losing the battle for public space. The thrusting of young people into more 'appropriate' spaces (such as youth centres) is restricting their ability to freely come together and hang out. Yet, if a young person hopes to maintain their networks and create new ones, they must have the places in which to do so. The spaces in which young people congregate are more than just places in which to 'hang out' and see friends, but instead provide young people with the ability to articulate appropriate cultural understanding and earn social worth.

No place of their own

Some would suggest that young people are provided with plenty of options in which to hang out. There are parks, youth centres, sporting venues and the like, which have been specifically provided for young people to congregate and hang out. So what is the problem with the spaces currently being provided for young people? The answer rests not on the type of spaces being provided, but on the dynamics existing within these spaces.

Children and young people have not featured prominently in the studies of geographers and where studies have been conducted, they focused on young people and children as future adults rather than as active agent in their own right (Mathews and Limb, 1999). As a result, much of the literature on community space and its use ignores the needs of children and young people. Young people are seldom deemed to be mature enough by adults to be outdoors on their own. In Australia as in much of the world, it could be argued that one of the few exceptions to this rule are natural open spaces such as nature parks and the beach;

DOI: 10.1057/9781137379702.0013

however, this may have more to do with the fact that these paces are more removed from the social forms of production and consumption than for their relative safety.[2] Adults attempt to keep young people out of harm by increasing surveillance through the provision of 'youth friendly spaces'. Youth friendly spaces are those spaces where the 'general atmosphere is one in which young people are treated with respect and dignity, and where they feel safe, secure and welcome' (Venkatesh and Kassimir, 2007, p. 232).

While placing young people into these spaces may remove them from the streets and provide some sense of security for community and parents alike, for young people in general youth friendly spaces may not provide suitable environments in which to freely network. For the most part, many of these spaces are set up to attempt to curb and control what is seen to be 'at risk behaviour' such as smoking, drinking and sexual activity through behaviour surveillance and censure. However, for young people, this type of censuring may not only feel inappropriate (after all, no one tells their parents that they must not smoke, drink or have sex!) but may in fact have dire consequences on their ability to network and accrue social capital.

Instead young people often discuss the need for youth specific spaces, These spaces allow them to be highly visible and to be part of the 'hustle and bustle' of their communities, provide entertainment, offer an exciting meeting place in which young people can be 'seen to be seen' and where they can create valuable social capital of their own. The search for youth specific spaces has led many young people to create new places in virtual social space. For young people, the internet and social networking sites present an opportunity to interact with peers, reinforce pre-existing friendships and allow for a rich extension of existing offline social networks outside adult surveillance and control.

Yet, the explosive growth of internet use by young people, together with the lack of control measures and a deficiency in parental computer confidence, has led to a steady stream of moral panics directed at internet use. Chief amongst these are the fears of online predators and cyber-bullying, heralded by the media as primary dangers for child and youth internet users. The exponential rise of internet use by young people has also seen an increase in allegations by the educational and psychological sector that too much time spent online can have other more direct negative effects, such as those listed by Mythil et al. (2008), who claim that increased exposure to the internet can have ill effects on

DOI: 10.1057/9781137379702.0013

school performance, impede adolescent achievement of psychosocial developmental tasks and lead to increased social isolation. As such, there is a strong movement toward the regularisation and surveillance of the internet, which could essentially replicate the many problems young people are facing in the physical world.

Addressing lack of place and space for young people

The conflict between young people and adults for the right to use space seems to be a widespread phenomenon among communities (Percy-Smith, 2002 and 2004; Valentine, 2004), an issue which at times can seem too daunting to tackle. Increasingly young people are either shunned from public space altogether or are presented with commercial public space as venues in which to network (only to find that they are in fact unwelcome unless they can also participate as consumers). This has meant that the rights of young people to gather together in public space are slowly being eroded, often resulting in young people meeting with resistance and sometimes open antagonism, leading to clashes between young people and adults.

The tensions created by these clashes can have severe repercussions on young people's ability to engage in meaningful dialogue with adults over their use of space. Adults often perceive young people, and their behaviour in social space, in terms of a problem to be solved through adult control. This need for control is then reproduced spatially within neighbourhoods (Percy-Smith, 2004) by the creation of boundaries, through surveillance and restriction of movement, in which young people are expected to comply with adult expectations of appropriate behaviour so as not to disturb the 'moral' and 'social' order (Valentine, 1996). This separation further exacerbates the disconnection between young people and adults, undermining any possibilities for dialogue on the shared use of space. The constant clashes and negative interactions between young people and adults in public space have meant that young people are faced with the challenge of growing up in a culture that has widespread negative perceptions of youth. This can undermine community cohesion by lowering the levels of trust between young people and adults and produce negative effects on young people's social capital, making it much harder for them to create meaningful bridging networks with the adult community.

DOI: 10.1057/9781137379702.0013

Conclusion

As has been discussed, young people and adults have been locked in a struggle for power over public space and its use. This struggle has often meant that young people are seen as undesirables within these spaces resulting in mistrust, resentment and a general lack of spaces in which they can gather and create social capital. Thus the dilemma before us is deciphering how to effectively respond to, and deal with, the conflict which arises between young people and adults when sharing public space. While the simple answer would be to create dialogue, this may at times be extremely complicated. Simply discussing issues arising from the use of space may not be sufficient to deal with the deep-rooted issues and tensions that lead to conflict over public space in communities. In cases where conflict arises, dominant groups will seek to control the use of space in ways that legitimise their views, interests and power over decision-making (Percy-Smith, 2004) and the imposition of dominant group's expectations of 'acceptable' behaviours in shared spaces.

Consequently, care must be taken when engaging young people in community discussions about shared use of space. Young people often complain that when they are invited to participate in consultation about the use of social space this is often done in a tokenistic fashion with their views either ignored or simply not tolerated (Percy-Smith, 2002 and 2006). Too often engagement in dialogue with young people is undertaken from the perspective of 'adult knows best', with little consideration that adults' perceptions of young people's needs may not correspond with reality (Percy-Smith et al., 2003; Percy-Smith and Weil, 2003; Percy-Smith, 2004). While providing young people with the opportunity to engage with adults in dialogue about the use of space is a positive step, any discussion should also include the opportunity for young people to create actual change (De Winter, 1997; Percy-Smith, 2006). When provision cannot be made for their needs, young people should be made aware of these shortcomings, and consultation should be undertaken to find a solution to ensure that young people's needs are not lost or marginalised within the more powerful adult agendas.

In short, we must acknowledge and respect that young people as members of our communities have a right to public space. They are a part of society and as such should be able to enjoy the benefits of our cities and towns and should be consulted on its use. For young people to form social capital they must network and be 'seen to be seen'. Young

DOI: 10.1057/9781137379702.0013

people require places in which to come together to socialise, create new friendships and most importantly accrue social capital. If we are to support the creation of youth social capital then spaces in which to network outside adult surveillance must be provided and a proactive approach to creating youth specific environments is needed. Young people must be engaged in the conversation by local councils and town planners in order to ensure that the needs of the diverse youth cultures are met. Establishing a conversation between young people and adults can have an added benefit. Not only will the outcome of conversations lead to an enhancement to both services and spaces available to young people, but it will also help to enhance the networking between young people and adults, leading to better inter-age connectedness and community cohesion.

Notes

1   Social capital refers to the combined (actual or potential) resources existing within networks (Bourdieu, 1986). In terms of young people, the social capital in friendships provides them with strong bonds which help them to navigate life by affording a sense of security, community, identity and belonging.
2   For a discussion on natural spaces and social relation of production, please see Lefebvre (1991).

DOI: 10.1057/9781137379702.0013

9

'Mum, if you've got a doctor's appointment take me or my sister': Contributions of a Child Language Broker

Siân Lucas

▶

Abstract: *This chapter explores the child language brokering experiences of a 17 year old British–Pakistani young person, fluent in English and Urdu, who regularly interprets, translates and mediates for her non-English speaking family members. The chapter illustrates the different components of child language brokering that include: interpretation, translation, mediation, organisational duties and decision-making. These components demonstrate how child language brokering facilitates communication between adults that do not share a common language and enables non-English speaking family members to access resources and information in the community. Child language brokering offers an understanding of the diversity of childhoods and families in contemporary society and the ways in which young people contribute to families and society.*

Joanne Westwood, Cath Larkins, Dan Moxon, Yasmin Perry and Nigel Thomas. *Participation, Citizenship and Intergenerational Relations in Children and Young People's Lives: Children and Adults in Conversation.* Basingstoke: Palgrave Macmillan. DOI: 10.1057/9781137379702.0014.

DOI: 10.1057/9781137379702.0014

Introduction

This chapter considers child language brokering (CLB), the process where children/young people interpret, translate and mediate for their non-English-speaking family members and other adults in private and public spheres. It is organised in the following way: firstly, I provide an overview of the key debates associated with CLB. Secondly, I present a portrait of Simran,[1] a 17-year-old British-Pakistani young person,[2] with experience of language brokering for her family members. I illustrate some of the ways that Simran benefits the collective needs of her family and society through language brokering, which includes: linguistic mediation, emotional support, organisational duties and decision-making.

The chapter adopts a social constructionist framework, following the work of James and Prout (1990; 1997). In this vein CLB offers a way to recognise the diversity of childhoods and families in contemporary society. I argue that child language brokers are active participants who use their knowledge to facilitate their families' access to resources and information (Orellana et al., 2003). I also demonstrate that Simran's positionality as a young person circumscribes the role she plays within the family and society and moreover contests compartmentalised understandings of appropriate roles and responsibilities, within the generational ordering of society (Christensen and Prout, 2003).

Child language brokering

CLB can be understood as a socio-cultural activity that involves some form of interpretation or translation with the child acting as the broker between adults that do not share a mutual language (Reynolds and Orellana, 2009). It is different to simply being bilingual, as it involves a 'constellation of practices' (Orellana, 2009, p. 61) in which children draw upon their linguistic, cultural and institutional knowledge to interpret, translate and mediate for family members and other adults in a number of different settings both inside and outside of the household that include: i) moments of crisis; ii) families seeking goods and services in the world outside their homes; and iii) quotidian ways both inside and outside the home (Orellana et al., 2003).

It is likely that CLB has occurred for centuries, throughout the world and linguistic groups, both spoken and signed. This will include

DOI: 10.1057/9781137379702.0014

children that have recently migrated, children classified as 'refugees' or 'asylum seekers' and children born in the country.[3] Nevertheless CLB is understood to be an 'invisible' or unrecognised area of childhood (Hall and Sham, 2007), which will be discussed later in the chapter. CLB is a relatively new area of research, which became a topic of research interest from the 1980s on. The extant research has explored different facets of CLB, which include: the experience of CLB in different institutions at, such as school parent evenings, with the GP and at the hospital (Cohen et al., 1999; García Sánchez and Orellana, 2006; Meyer et al., 2010); different perspectives of CLB, for example, bilingual and monolingual young people and parents (Cline et al., 2011; Morales et al., 2012); and the effects of CLB, for example, the relationship between CLB and behavioural and emotional development, depression and self-efficacy (Buriel, 1998; Buriel et al., 2006; Martinez et al., 2009).

CLB is conceptualised as a family practice (Martinez et al., 2009) in which families pool their skills and resources across generations (Orellana, Reynolds et al., 2003). It has been associated with the overall well-being of the family and identified as a significant feature in the adjustment to a new host country and integration in society (Suárez-Orozco and Suárez-Orozco, 2001) and, as we will see, for children born in the country. Candappa and Igbinigie (2003) found that young refugees in London used their language proficiency to communicate directly with officials; in one case this enabled the family to remain in the United Kingdom. Parents in a study by Morales et al. (2012) expressed a preference for their children to language broker rather than external interpreters and language brokering was seen to strengthen family bonds.

Despite such contributions, it has been noted that children do not perceive their language brokering to be the most helpful activity performed in the family (Orellana, 2009; Villanueva and Buriel, 2010). This corresponds with a recurrent theme of the literature: that children conceptualise language brokering as a normal and unremarkable part of everyday life, 'not a source of pride but a fact of life' (Cline et al., 2011, p. 218).

CLB is reported to have a number of benefits and is believed to improve children's syntactical and lexical development (Orellana, 2009), student academic performance (Buriel, 1998; Orellana, 2003) and the development and reinforcement of children's ethnic identity and cultural values (Weisskirch et al., 2011). Kaur and Mills (2002, p. 125) found that 'young

DOI: 10.1057/9781137379702.0014

interpreters' experienced places and knowledge 'prematurely', which led to 'increased maturity, astuteness, assertiveness and self-reliance, born of early adult experience'.

Specific stressors associated with CLB have also been presented by a number of researchers; these debates are situated within wider questions about typical and atypical work of children within the family. Firstly, Mcquillan and Tse (1995) found that some language brokers found language brokering to be stressful, Weisskirch and Alva (2002) refer to CLB as 'an age-graded phenomenon', meaning that younger children in the early stages of language and cognitive development may find language brokering more stressful than adolescents (Buriel et al., 2006). Secondly, the context of CLB is said to influence young people's experiences of CLB; Villanueva and Buriel (2010) found that students experienced a heightened sense of stress during parents' evening, particularly if they were communicating poor performance to their parents; similarly Hall and Sham (2007) reported that children found language brokering stressful, while working in the family take-away business. Thirdly, a number of researchers have identified concern about accuracy, particularly in medical appointments and at the hospital (Cohen et al., 1999; Meyer et al., 2010). Fourthly, CLB is associated with 'parentification' (Walsh et al., 2006) or role-reversal (Candappa and Egharevba, 2002), based on the understanding that it is as a form of parental dependency, which erodes the hierarchical structure of the family and undermines parental authority.

These concerns have influenced some institutions to discourage the practice of CLB or family interpreters, for instance, the London Child Protection Procedures (HMSO, 2011) advise that children should not interpret for family members (section: 50.5.4). Despite such guidance, we know that public service institutions face fiscal and structural challenges and that 'professional' adult interpreters are not always available (Meyer et al., 2010). This disparity points to the essential role of CLB, and moreover may explain why CLB is an 'invisible' area of childhood.

CLB disturbs traditional understandings of the family, in which the majority of family decisions and responsibilities are divided between parents, and children's work is classified into typical and atypical work (Mayall, 2002a) which excludes them from certain activities, opportunities and experiences (Crafter et al., 2009). CLB encourages us to recognise the diverse ways that families function in society, including the division of tasks within the family, individual family dynamics and family structure

DOI: 10.1057/9781137379702.0014

(Thorne, 1982; Lamb, 1999; Erera, 2002). Eksner and Orellana (2012, p. 200) propose that CLB challenges models of expert-novice relationships and 'in language brokering events, knowledge is located both within and between the brokering child and the parent-interlocutor'.

Although it may appear that the child represents the 'voice' of their parents, Eksner and Orellana (2012) argue that knowledge and authority are shared and negotiated among children and parents to achieve common goals. Children act under the direct supervision of their parents, who provide 'scaffolding' support, particularly in written translation tasks by breaking up translations, intercepting and instructing. Parents also used the brokering experience in a pragmatic way, to encourage and improve the child's home language. This can be attributed to findings from Valdez (2003) who argues that CLB does not compromise parental authority and children conform to traditional childhood roles, that is, respect and obedience to adults even though language brokering alters traditional parent-child relationships.

This section has demonstrated some of the key debates and complexities associated with CLB. As mentioned earlier, the phenomenon of CLB presents a way to recognise the social construction of the family, in which children carry out 'adult roles'. It is important to note that Orellana (2009) has critiqued the tendency of researchers to conceptualise CLB as negative/positive due to the variability of CLB experiences on the individual child and family. This chapter attempts to avoid this binary logic and does not make generalised claims about CLB experiences per se; rather, I present insight into the CLB experiences of one young person to contribute to the existing knowledge about the multifaceted nature of CLB that includes organising, advocating and decision-making.

The project

I explored CLB as part of my doctoral studies, through a qualitative study that explored bilingual (taken to mean fluency in two or more languages) young people's experiences of language brokering for their family members. The fieldwork took place at a youth centre[4] in 'Hillshire', an anonymised ward within a town in West Yorkshire, over a period of three months and involved interviews with nine young people aged 12–17 years. The young people had resided in England for different lengths of time; four were born in England and used English, Urdu and Punjabi.

DOI: 10.1057/9781137379702.0014

The five other young people had migrated with their families to England in the past 5 years from the Czech Republic.[5]

I have chosen to present a portrait of one of these young people, Simran, a 17-year-old female with experience of language brokering for her family members. There are two main reasons for the focus on Simran; firstly, she offers rich descriptions and a nuanced understanding of what CLB involves, means and does for her family. Secondly, existing CLB research focuses on children that have recently migrated and are learning a new system. Simran however is a British citizen, born in England; her CLB experience may be transferrable for other British child language brokers.

The following section begins with a portrait of Simran, using the theme of intergenerationality, taken to mean the way Simran interacts and provides linguistic and cultural mediation for her family, horizontally (for her siblings) and vertically (across older generations). I present excerpts from an interview with Simran to demonstrate how intergenerationality is entwined in the language brokering encounter, which involves two key components: i) organising and ii) advocating and problem solving.

A portrait of Simran

Simran is a 17-year-old female, born in Hillshire, to parents of Pakistani descent.[6] She is bilingual and uses English, Punjabi and Urdu in her daily life; she has language brokered for her mother and grandfather since the age of 12 and shares this task with her younger sister. Simran's language brokering experience covers the three categories outlined by Orellana, Dorner et al. (2003), which include:

- ‣ responding to telephone calls with the school and other bodies;
- ‣ arranging medical appointments for the family;
- ‣ translating letters; and
- ‣ attending planned and ad-hoc appointments at the GP and hospital.

Organising

The act of translating letters addressed to different members of the family is one example of Simran's organisational contributions. Simran and her

DOI: 10.1057/9781137379702.0014

family work collectively to ensure that her mother has the linguistic support she requires to make sure that appointments and institutional demands are kept. Simran uses linguistic knowledge to translate the letters from English into Urdu to ensure her mother understands the content and is aware of events in the community around her. Letters include: bank statements, letters from the GP/school and promotional literature that advertise local sales and community events.

Simran responds to letters in four stages. Firstly, she opens the letters addressed to all household members; she discards letters that don't require attention and group letters that need to be translated. Secondly, Simran translates and discusses the content with her mother. Thirdly, Simran responds to the letters, autonomously and collaboratively, with her mother's instructions and marks appointments and events on the family calendar. The fourth step involves input from adult family members (paternal auntie and father), who retain authorial control by checking through the letters and responding to the letters that Simran has not opened. This four-stage process can be resembled as a type of 'workplace' that involves the co-ordination of activities and household chores between family members (Hochschild, 2003; Morrow, 2011). Members of the family use a calendar to ensure that appointments are kept and check their diaries so that Simran's mother has a family member to language broker for her when she needs it.

Advocating and problem solving

As mentioned earlier, language brokering involves more than bilingualism; in Simran's case it can also include organisational duties, advocating (as we will see shortly) and problem solving.

Simran has language brokered for over five years in a number of different settings. She organises her language brokering schedule in accordance with her knowledge of linguistic resources within the community; she knows where interpreters will and won't be. Simran has the experience and confidence to speak with professionals in a variety of settings and has insight into institutional processes, such as the likely questions, dialogue and procedures that characterise specific contexts. This experience has enhanced Simran's confidence to ask for clarification and challenge professionals when necessary as outlined in the following example at the community nursery.

DOI: 10.1057/9781137379702.0014

[B]ecause the [nursery staff] are mainly English ... they speak fluent English and my mum didn't know that, so she tried to understand ... but she didn't so she took me to help. Their English was too hard for her to understand, there were some words for me to understand hard ... I asked [the Nursery Assistant], they explain what they mean to me.

Simran has the knowledge and empathy to recognise the extent of her mother's English language comprehension and she has the confidence to request for clarification. Simran juxtaposes her personal English language proficiency to emphasise that the misunderstanding was not entirely down to her mother's proficiency of English, but rather related to the professional's lexicon and presumably that interpreters were unavailable. Again she summarises the experience and the action taken to mitigate the difficulty. The excerpt infers to different types of English proficiency; Simran alludes that her mother understands some English, but not 'fluent English'. It is important to note Simran's positioning of language in the past tense, her mother 'didn't know' English rather than 'does not' in the present tense. Although the accuracy of this statement cannot be guaranteed, it reminds us that language proficiency is not static and that significant numbers of people are learning English (Tse, 2001). The excerpt can be related to findings from Villanueva and Buriel (2010), who saw parents preferred their children to language broker, with the intention that the child would develop and maintain dual language proficiency, and because they were reluctant to speak English due to their 'heavy' English accents.

In the following excerpt Simran discusses how she advocates and resolves a particular issue concerned with her sister, who had been involved in an accident. Simran talks about an ad-hoc language brokering experience, in which she makes the decision to intercept a telephone call between her mother and the GP receptionist. While the focus of the telephone is to gain medical attention, the excerpt exposes the linguistic marginalisation of her mother and the way Simran acts on her own volition and according to cues from her mother to advocate and overcome these challenges.

[M]y mum phoned [the surgery] and [tried to explain what had happened, but] ... they put the phone down. I rung, I got really angry, I said my mum just phoned and you put the phone down ... and they said um 'oh sorry we didn't understand what she was saying'. I said you know what, if you don't understand, just explain to her; wait for someone else to come. And I went really angry, I flipped on her, I shouldn't have like flipped on her. I explained

DOI: 10.1057/9781137379702.0014

what happened and said you're not taking it seriously, [the receptionist] put me on hold so I rang again, I said I want to talk to my GP was our own man, the same race, I got my mum, I said you speak to him and tell them what happened.

The excerpt shows the intergenerational nature of the context that involves Simran, her sister and mother; she expresses embedded alliance to her family and understanding of the world from the perspective of her mother as an adult with limited English language proficiency. Simran's cultural knowledge tells her the receptionist shouldn't hang up and she has the confidence to advocate by way of challenging the receptionist to ensure that her mother speaks with the GP, hence protecting the dignity of her mother and the well-being of her sister. By doing so she calls into question the receptionist's professional (and moral) responsibility to respond to patients and realigns the professional procedure. From a structural level, this exposes the institutional challenges of public welfare services to meet the needs of the multilingual population (Green et al., 2005); it can be associated with wider language ideologies and illusory notions of correctness, based on language varieties and linguistic difference (Milroy and Milroy, 1999; Lippi-Green, 1997; Blackledge, 2004; Garrett, 2010).

It is interesting to trace the narrative of the episode; it begins with her mother's individual attempt to contact the GP and Simran's intervention when she realises her mother is experiencing difficulties. Given that Simran has the linguistic faculty, cultural and situational knowledge to speak personally, she pursues her mothers' attempts to speak directly with a medical professional. This indicates that Simran has an understanding of the limits of agency as a language broker; she provides intergenerational support by focussing on the well-being of her sister and hence respects and asserts the social status and authorial command of her mother. In a similar way to the former excerpts, the narrative leans towards the finality of the encounter; the end point in which Simran successfully arranges for her mother to speak with the GP. These examples show that Simran uses 'interactional logic' (Alanen, 2001) to carry out organisational tasks, particularly decision-making within the parameters of parental authority. The ending point of this encounter, particularly Simran's relief to speak with her 'own man' highlights relief borne of not only linguistic membership but also in regards to racial affiliation. This affirms Simran's awareness of linguistic, cultural and racial divides, in this case marked by the distinction 'race'. Finally

DOI: 10.1057/9781137379702.0014

Simran reflects upon the experience. Following her understanding of politeness and expected behaviour (Spencer-Oatey, 2008; Mills, 2003), she manages her feelings and recognises that she shouldn't have 'flipped' on the receptionist. While she notes anger, she rationalises this with the magnitude of the situation and the need for her mother to speak with the GP.

In the final excerpt, Simran displays linguistic and emotional empathy toward her mother. Again, akin to the nursery incident, the language choices of the GP are referred to. This reminds us that it is Simran's mother's language proficiency that is the central foci. Simran and realises she doesn't need to translate verbatim, as it is unnecessary that she understands every word of the interaction.

> [S]o my mum goes in [to the surgery]...[the GP's] trying to explain, she doesn't understand, she goes: I'll call my daughter, so my mum calls me and then [the GP] explains it in detail so I try to understand some of the doctor's...words (laugh), I can't explain each little word cos I didn't get what they mean...after we were there...we said if you've got a doctor's appointment take me or my sister, other than that don't, don't go.

The finality of Simran's advice to her mother reinforces the reality and complexity of CLB: it is preferable for Simran or her sister to broker for her mother rather than her mother going alone, and Simran feels she has the authority to assert this ultimatum.

The components of the language brokering experience, organising, advocating and problem solving, allude to the ways that young people are active participants and contribute to the well-being and functioning of the family and society (Hall and Sham, 2007; Suárez-Orozco and Suárez-Orozco, 1995).

Before ending this section it is important to consider agency. As Mayall (2002b, p. 21) reminds us, 'Childhood agency has to be understood within the parameters of childhood's minority status' in which adults hold authority over children in some way – politically, economically and financially – and hence children are both vehicles for transmitting information and objects of evaluation. While Simran expresses family allegiance she reminds us there are limits to her agency; she knows which letters she should and shouldn't open and will seek advice from adult members and other artefacts (Google translate/dictionaries) if she is unsure about certain issues/terminology. As CLB is a family practice and children's worlds are generationally structured (Alanen, 2001)

DOI: 10.1057/9781137379702.0014

Simran shares the language brokering with her English-speaking auntie, sister and father to ensure that her mother has necessary linguistic support. There are occasions where Simran does not language broker for her mother; as the earlier excerpt demonstrates, this can be a strategic decision, to highlight institutional deficiencies and to encourage and enable her mother to speak for herself. This uncovers deep complexities and pragmatic challenges; it appears that there is a linguistic expectation on the GP. This highlights the untenable situation of minority ethnic staff and their expectation to represent and support the minority ethnic community (Lewis, 2000; Williams and Johnson, 2010). While the chapter focuses on the language brokering experience, it is important to note the multiple factors that are likely to affect the CLB experience, which include: class, race, ethnicity, religion, gender, education and socio-economic status (Crenshaw, 1989; Collins, 1980).

Conclusion

This chapter has explored the experience of Simran, a young person who 'language brokers' for her family members. I have shown that CLB involves more than fluency in multiple languages and involves actions in the front and back regions (Goffman, 1969), which include acquiescence, responding and waiting for instruction, discussions with parents, as well as organisational skills, problem solving and advocating. The chapter demonstrates that child language brokers not only have a sophisticated understanding of multiple languages but they also know how to navigate a myriad of systems, besides having knowledge of institutional resources and an understanding of the institutional barriers that face members of the population on the basis of their language proficiency. While the contributions of CLB are significant, it raises important implications: firstly, child language brokers expose deficiencies in public services' capacity to provide appropriate linguistic services; we can see that Simran's mother is dependent on familial resources that compensate for unresponsive mainstream services (Chahal, 2004). By identifying Simran's language brokering we see how her everyday actions contribute to the social and economic health and well-being of her family and the society. Finally, the research provides an alternative understanding of the conceptualisation of intergenerationality and highlights the diversity of roles that children undertake within the family and society. Given

DOI: 10.1057/9781137379702.0014

continued migration patterns, CLB offers fertile ground for inquiry across the globe.

Acknowledgements

This research was funded by the ESRC: ES/H023720/1. I would like to thank the youth centre staff, Simran and all of the young people who took time to participate in the research. I would also like to thank the reviewers for their helpful comments and colleagues at UCLA, in particular Marjorie Faulstich Orellana for her comments on an earlier version of this chapter.

Notes

1   For confidentiality purposes pseudonyms are used, and these names were chosen by the participants. The project was approved by the University of Salford Ethics & Governance Committee.

2   Throughout the chapter I refer to children and young people interchangeably.

3   In this respect I am referring to England; however this could apply to countries throughout the globe.

4   The youth centre is managed by the local authority and is attended by Pakistani and Czech young people. Hillshire is one of the most deprived wards of the town, characterised by high density, with high levels of unemployment and poor educational attainment.

5   Hillshire has been home to a number of minority groups over the past century, from Ireland, Pakistan and in more recent years Central and Eastern Europe. Pakistanis are the largest minority ethnic group in Hillshire (5.3 per cent) and Islam is the second most prevalent religion after Christianity. The ethnic make-up of the youth centre and Hillshire is important to outline; the youth workers were predominantly female British-Pakistani and interacted with the young people in English and Urdu. This is not characteristics of wider public services in Hillshire where 87 per cent of staff is white British.

6   Simran is a Sunni-Muslim; her mother and grandparents were born in the Mirpur region of Pakistan.

DOI: 10.1057/9781137379702.0014

10
Change-scape Theory: Applications in Participatory Practice

Vicky Johnson

▶ **Abstract:** *This chapter explores a model developed from case study research carried out in Nepal and the United Kingdom. It argues that children's participation should be seen to take place in the space of 'Change-scapes' that show the mechanisms through which this participation can change the context in which they live. The extent of this change depends on how different stakeholders, including adults in communities, are involved in the process. Creating or using existing participatory spaces that encourage participation and dialogue while employing mechanisms for communication and collaborative approaches can shift power dynamics, lead to a better understanding of children's lives and change attitudes and behaviours. Through training, capacity can be built and staff and decision-makers develop trust in young people's evidence and roles in participatory processes.*

Joanne Westwood, Cath Larkins, Dan Moxon, Yasmin Perry and Nigel Thomas. *Participation, Citizenship and Intergenerational Relations in Children and Young People's Lives: Children and Adults in Conversation.* Basingstoke: Palgrave Macmillan. DOI: 10.1057/9781137379702.0015.

 DOI: 10.1057/9781137379702.0015

Introduction

This chapter first introduces a Change-scape framework that was developed through re-visiting participatory processes with children and young people in the United Kingdom and Nepal (Johnson 2010a, 2010b, 2011). This Change-scape represents the connections between cultural, political and physical context and children and young people's participation, and as such highlights the importance of their interaction with different stakeholders including their peers, adults in local communities and local decision-makers. Ideas from this theoretical framework have been transferred into practice in training and application of children and young people's participation in Peru, Ethiopia and Sierra Leone (Johnson et al., 2013); learning from these processes is shared in this chapter.

The three main mechanisms that are discussed in this chapter in the context of the application of the Change-scape in practice are as follows:

1   Communication and collaboration between adults and children involved in participatory processes is key to long-lasting change. In different cultural and political contexts, there may be different mechanisms to encourage communication that in turn shifts adult attitudes towards children's roles and power dynamics.
2   In order to include different children who may have different perceptions of their identity and have varying interest in participating, spaces for their participation will need to be considered.
3   Continuity and sustainability may be achieved through capacity-building of staff and adults in the community as well as children who want to be involved. 'Champions for children' can help to energize and sustain more meaningful participation and action.

Background: Change-scape theory

The Change-scape is based on linking children to their context and raising issues of power and spaces for participation as important processes of children and young people's participation. The mechanisms that help to link children to their context are: improved communication and collaboration between children and adults involved in the processes, including those in positions of power making decision; recognising the power

DOI: 10.1057/9781137379702.0015

dynamics and spaces that exist and can be created for children's participation; ensuring there is adequate capacity-building and that champions for children's participation are identified. Mechanisms that lead to children and young people's participation becoming more meaningful in participatory processes can achieve more sustainable change and transformation for children and organisations working to improve their lives.

This Change-scape was developed through case study research, revisiting participatory processes in Nepal and the United Kingdom to understand where, when and how children and young people's perceptions and evidence had been taken seriously and whether this had led to transformational change on an individual, organisational or societal level. In different contexts, change for children and young people and for organisations was examined, and conditions for change understood more fully. Even at a societal level, with adequate support and continued commitment from different stakeholders, there was found to be significant shifts in attitudes and behaviours of adults and decision-makers towards children under specific circumstances. Lessons were drawn from the case studies visited in non-governmental and government organisations in Nepal and the United Kingdom. The Change-scape was formulated using the following theoretical perspectives and has continued to develop with application in different field situations.

The 'Change-scape' was constructed using cultural- and socio-ecological theories following Vygotsky that connect children to their context over time, specifically Bronfenbrenner, 1979, 2005; Tudge, 2008). Children are connected to different significant other players in a particular context through bi-directional proximal processes. In the Change-scape the children and young people are affected by their context, but there is also recognition that they can change their context – this is represented by two-way arrows on the Change-scape. Recent socio-ecological theories do not place children at the centre, but connect children to processes, context and time in a more fluid and organic way (Bronfenbrenner, 2005; Tudge and Hogan, 2005). I have placed children and young people as central, highlighting their importance and the imperative for their centrality in decision-making processes that affect their lives and that fits with rights-based approaches. The visual of children at the centre is also easier for many organisations to take on board.

Children and young people at the centre of the Change-scape involves their identity, inclusion and interest in participatory processes. In the original construction of the Change-scape the identity and interest of

DOI: 10.1057/9781137379702.0015

children was specified, but as the framework has developed inclusion has been added as an important additional concept when considering how to include different children and young people in processes. How children construct their identity is an important starting point for inclusive children's participation (also see Mannion, 2010). There are structural determinants of inequality that intersect and mean that different children of different age, gender, ethnicity/ caste, religion and so on are included in society and in decision-making processes in different ways. Local power dynamics are key to understanding how different children may participate and what their interest in a process may be. It is an ethical issue whether children take up their right to participate and they need to be given the space to opt out of participatory processes with dignity.

The importance of the changing political economy and analysis of cultural beliefs and institutional context arose from the case study research as key driving forces for, or barriers to, local change to improve children's well-being. Different levels of resources and continued support or commitment to children's agency also made a difference to changing attitudes and aspirations amongst children and adults. Mechanisms or strategies of communication and collaboration between different stakeholders and the creation of better spaces for children's participation determined the extent to which decision-makers valued (or did not value) children's evidence in decisions. A 'Change-scape' framework (see Figure 10.1) was created in order to analyse this relationship between

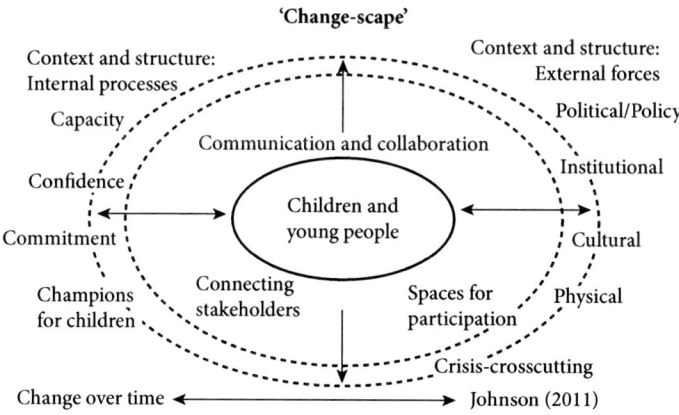

FIGURE 10.1   *Change-scape*

DOI: 10.1057/9781137379702.0015

context and process. Concepts of critical realism and real world research (e.g., Robson, 2002) helped to understand how context could link to processes and how different mechanisms could translate outcomes into action that could be positive for children and young people.

The case study research carried out in Nepal and the United Kingdom that led to the construction of the 'Change-scape' provided evidence showing that the way in which children participate can change the context in which they live. The extent of this change depends on how different stakeholders, including adults in communities, are involved in the process. Creating or using existing participatory spaces that encourage participation and dialogue while employing mechanisms for communication and collaborative approaches can shift power dynamics, lead to a better understanding of children's lives and change attitudes and behaviours. This has parallels with Corsaro's (1992) interpretive reproduction in children's peer cultures.

The following sections of the chapter draw on both experiences from the case study research and the application of the Change-scape theory in practice in working with local partners of an international children's charity called ChildHope UK in Ethiopia, Peru and Sierra Leone.

Communication and collaboration between adults and children

Working *with*, rather than *for*, children, that is, treating children as active participants rather than recipients of interventions and action, requires shifts in attitudes from those in positions of power. This may become even more profound as children take on different roles in participatory processes, as leaders and designers of research and learning. One of the core principles of participatory appraisal training and learning is to change attitudes and behaviour of those people in communities who hold power (e.g., Kumar, 1996). If policy and practice does not change, including financial and human resource policy and implementation, then children and young people's participation may be tokenistic.

Examples from the case study research in Nepal and the United Kingdom showed that the level of involvement that children had in the form of dialogue with service providers and decision-makers made a difference to how their contributions were valued. Sometimes shifts in cultural, political and institutional power dynamics were too great to change the minds of all the decision-makers involved and children's perspectives merely satisfied central government or donor requirements to consult. Mechanisms or strategies of increased communication and dialogue, and being creative about the different spaces for participation in communities and institutions, however, started to shift some of the preconceived ideas about the capabilities and roles of girls, boys, young women and men, and to change some of the minds of people in positions of power.

Processes carried out in Ethiopia, Peru and Sierra Leone therefore prioritized increasing communication between people that may be involved in changing children's lives locally. Training and workshops created spaces where children and adults worked together to discuss barriers and facilitators for children and young people's participation in their local communities and to develop a local action plan. Any of these training workshops were also seen as integrated into a process of longer term learning, changing institutional policies and challenging attitudes of staff and adult volunteers within the communities. Children's participation was also therefore examined within an organisation's theory of change and ongoing organisational development. In creating constructive training in children's participation, we may also need to shift our understanding of pedagogy, drawing on UNESCO's pillars, from 'learning to know', to also 'learning how to be, do, and live together' (Thomson et al., 2012). If training involves staff, adults and decision-makers from the community as well as children, then preconceptions about children's capabilities and roles can be confronted and challenged. Training needs to address how local realities and action planning are embedded in cultural contexts and how children's participation can seek to transform not only individuals and organisations, but also attitudes and beliefs about children in broader society.

To encourage deeper thinking about children and young people's participation, staff in an organisation can be involved in creating a change in attitudes towards children and young people and in generating more dialogue between adults and children in communities. Children and young people's participation training in ChildHope UK involved running a five-day workshop on understanding children and young people's participation and local action planning with children, teachers, social workers and community child rights advocates (see Johnson et al., 2013). Experienced local facilitators were trained as trainers so that training could be rolled out more broadly and children and young people's participation considered throughout the organisation over time.

DOI: 10.1057/9781137379702.0015

Rather than assuming that children and young people are homogenous, their identity, inclusion and interest, as suggested in the Change-scape, were taken into account to ensure that the most marginalized were reached in training, action planning and ongoing participatory work in communities. As children and young people's participation has become more visible or popular in broader international social development processes, in order to achieve meaningful outcomes for children, power dynamics evident in different contexts need to be recognised and addressed. Challenges may relate to broader contexts, including how to convince those people in positions of power to go beyond tokenism in children's participation, build on dialogical approaches and encourage innovative and flexible participatory processes with children and young people.

Creating participatory spaces for inclusion

Participatory spaces can encompass going out to where children and young people are rather than expecting them to enter more adult orientated spaces, also creating new spaces for participation that are child/young person friendly and promote dialogue with adults in communities and decision-makers (e.g., Cornwall, 2004; Kesby, 2005). Children's participation training can also build on ideas from Chambers (1983) in terms of moving away from development tourism, or White and Choudhury's (2007) analysis that suggests going out to where children are so that action planning with children is carried out on their terms and in their contexts. Therefore training workshops run by ChildHope were held within communities and local children were given space to build their confidence to work with local adults and decision-makers from the community. This process took time and different visual methods and games were employed to ensure that workshops were relevant but fun.

Examples of participatory spaces and dialogue encouraged in the case studies in Nepal and the United Kingdom included:

▶ Peer groups in which issues were discussed and action planned and evaluated
▶ Reference groups of service providers who are educated about children's involvement and evidence
▶ Showcases and visits of service providers and decision-makers to interact with children including presentation using different media

DOI: 10.1057/9781137379702.0015

▶ Informal lunches and networking events to stimulate dialogue between stakeholders including children and young people
▶ Feedback and dialogue sessions including children's clubs which may be supported by adults but run by children
▶ Supportive relationships such as mentoring provided by adults that can support children and young people when needed

Examples of creating participatory spaces in the workshop trainings in Ethiopia, Peru and Sierra Leone were: children working together on analysis; children taking adults out on guided walks; using skits and role plays to show different scenarios and power dynamics; co-constructing physical maps and photos of safe and unsafe areas for children, for example, where children's knowledge was shown to be vital to create the map. Local adults were often surprised by the degree of competency shown by children and young people. However, children, sometimes boys and girls separately, needed to work in separate groups on some issues to build up their confidence and ideas and to decide what and how they presented these to adults.

The idea of creating spaces for children in ongoing action planning was addressed in a training workshop held with children and adults from the local community, teachers and staff, working with a Sierra Leonean organisation: 'Streetchild of Sierra Leone'. Child clubs were seen as one way of allowing children space to work together, although these will also need to be monitored to see how seriously children's views are taken. Natasha Kwakwa Tesfai talks about what happened after one of the training workshops in Sierra Leone (Figure 10.2).

> The outcomes of initial community training with children, adults, teachers and staff, carried out for Street Child of Sierra Leone, are demonstrated by the increased activity of 'kids clubs' which have been set up in 17 schools, involving over 1000 children. Children in these clubs set their priorities for involvement in decision-making in school and home environment, including more autonomy to elect school prefects, more consultation over next-level school choices and the space to plan and carry out their own child rights advocacy. 'Kids clubs' members have reduced stigma and discrimination against children who have lived in the street or teenage mothers who have come back to school by organising debates and discussions on the topics and counseling peers. Children in these clubs have been pivotal in championing child rights, and children's responsibilities that go with rights, responding to tensions between traditional leaders and children, who complain of a loss of respect for elders. The challenges that the local organisation now faces are

DOI: 10.1057/9781137379702.0015

adapting ways of working, and securing resources to ensure that children participate in planning, implementing and monitoring activities that affect them.

Being immersed in participatory processes in ongoing interventions in Peru, one of the young women from the Andes region had the confidence

FIGURE 10.2   *Children and adults facilitating children in Sierra Leone*

DOI: 10.1057/9781137379702.0015

to share her experiences with young people from the United Kingdom in an international conference on children's participation, and many participants commented on how profound her contribution was to their thinking about participation in different parts of the world. One of the young people, Zoraida Mamani Rosado, aged 19, discusses her experiences of participating in the conference: Children, Young People and Adults: Extending the Conversation, Preston, United Kingdom, 2012.[1]

> Personally I feel very motivated because the conference was led by children...or young people. It was impressive to see how kind, participatory and respectful they all were. I loved the way they welcomed me. I struggled a bit in communicating with them due to the language barrier, but I felt more relaxed with the presence of the translator...I liked all the experiences that each of the young people shared with us, but what struck me more profoundly was the way they were paying attention to my own experiences, and the realities my country suffers. They showed interest and appreciation for what I had to say and who I am...I believe that keeping silence is not the way to solve problems; on the contrary it is through conversation and exchange of ideas that problems in every country can be solved. I hope the other participants take with them everything that I said, as I am taking with me some great moments and the experiences they shared with me.

Capacity-building and champions for children

Commitment and capacity of decision- and policy-makers can increase as confidence in children and young people's participation grows and their evidence is seen to be meaningful and worthwhile. For example, in one of the case studies revisited in the United Kingdom, members of the scheme's partnership board were divided in opinion about the value of children's evidence in evaluation until some of the members of the board saw that children offered a fresh perspective. With children's rigorous presentation of visual and audio evidence to back up the external evaluators' evidence, board members and service providers became more convinced of the value of children's input. Some of the service providers said that they needed to be convinced as they learnt new visual approaches and methods that helped them interact with children and their families in a meaningful way. Consequently some changed the way in which their service was delivered to incorporate the views of girls and boys who were at the receiving end of their programme. Evidence was collected in the case study research of changes of services and allocation of resources

DOI: 10.1057/9781137379702.0015

made on the basis of children's input to participatory evaluation processes. This process of moving from just capturing children's pictures, stories and quotes to influencing decision-making can be helped along by 'champions for children'. In the United Kingdom this proved to be mentors, senior members of partnership boards and heads of services; in Nepal, managers and researchers; and in one of the villages, it was a child member of the childclub who motivated peers to work with adults in their community in an innovative and structured way. He is now a local journalist.

In Ethiopia, a local organisation called CHADET (Organisation for Child Development and Transformation) identified that their work with girls migrating into cities from rural areas needed to be more sensitive to their participation. They were willing to understand how their organisation may need to change in order to do this. This process was encouraged and supported by Comic Relief who had recognized children's participation as one of CHADET's core organisational development goals. Allan Kiwanuka discusses the longer term implications of training with children, adults and staff from a local community in Arsela in Ethiopia:

> Building on initial training on children and young people's participation run by Vicky, the Organisation for Child Development and Transformation (CHADET - ChildHope's partner organisation in Ethiopia), organised a training of trainers in children's participation for an additional 70 staff from its Wolliso, Kombolcha and Debre Tabor project sites. It also developed an organisational Guideline on Children's Participation that includes children and adults from communities in community training including action planning to encourage children's participation in community decision-making.
>
> CHADET is an organisation working to improve the lives of girls migrating to cities from remote rural locations and have increased emphasis on children's involvement in identifying new project beneficiaries. Nearly 1,600 vulnerable out-of-school girls were identified by their peers, who are members of girls' school clubs supported by CHADET and have now been supported to resume school. These girls' clubs have played a key role in annulling arranged marriages for 52 girls with support of teachers and local child protection committees. The girls sent teams to parents, negotiated and convinced them to allow their peers to resume education. Some girls' clubs have amended their club laws to allow some boys to participate in their clubs because they say they need male actors during community awareness activities.
>
> Children's voices in project planning, monitoring and budgeting are also increasing. Two children's project management committees have been created at Kombolcha and Debra Tabor Woredas to ensure children's perspectives inform CHADET's field teams. They reviewed and made recommendations

DOI: 10.1057/9781137379702.0015

on CHADET's 2012 annual plan and budget. While disseminating results of a qualitative baseline survey carried out by CHADET in Debra Tabor (March 2012), the researcher reported that one child was forced to run away from home to streets after stealing nearly £2,900 from home. The children unanimously queried credibility of this finding because according to them: 'no household in our village has such large sums of money'.

Sharing knowledge and new ways of thinking about inclusion, rights, power, cultural and political context and participation need to underpin any children and young people's participation training. As discussed later, a range of models and theoretical frameworks can be utilised both with staff and facilitators planning training in local communities and with children and young people. Providing a range of theoretical inputs and frameworks allows facilitators of training sessions to select the aspects that will best suit their ongoing and longer term participatory work and context, thus giving more chance of long term sustainable change. It is also critical that training and 'training of trainers' processes allow facilitators and participants the space to develop their own frameworks and models of participation.

In Sierra Leone, staff discussed a range of concepts for their local trainings with staff, teachers, community adults and children. They wanted to include concepts from Berry Mayall's work (e.g., 2002b) on power dynamics between children and adults, and Mary Kellet's work (e.g., 2004) on children as researchers. A simple spectrum to consider whether we are working *for* children, *with* children or whether processes are carried out *by* children was found to be useful across all training programmes.

In Ethiopia, a workshop was run with orphans and vulnerable children as well as *Idir* (funeral society) leaders who have started to provide services for children. Facilitators chose to illustrate Hart's (1992) ladder of participation with different international and local examples of participatory processes. They drew out issues of whether or not children had initiated participatory processes into a participatory exercise with the group. The Change-scape was also used to explore what people locally meant by 'a child' or 'a young person', their identity, inclusion and interest in the processes of participation. Participants analysed the relevance of local cultural, political and institutional features of context that facilitate or hinder children and young people's participation.

Peruvian children suggested that theoretical input was necessary for them to understand fully the concept of children's participation and take ideas to their peers in order to put their training into practice. Peruvian

DOI: 10.1057/9781137379702.0015

colleagues also presented their own model of children's participation, discussed how models fitted together, and how one could modify ideas depending on practice and the different frameworks and concepts presented. Training can therefore start with a realisation that children and young people can engage in theoretical discussion.

> Presenting and discussing complex or abstract theories around children and young people's participation in a manner that is accessible and interesting for young people themselves was a challenging but necessary part of the training. Peruvian young people said that theories helped them to understand the ideas behind the issues in children's participation and essentially this would help them to pass on the knowledge they had learned to their peers. For them to gain full understanding of the theories, it was not enough to simply present and discuss them, it was essential to find innovate ways of exploring theories and to explain them in simple and accessible language with which diverse groups of participants can engage. By using dynamic and inclusive techniques to explore theories, children and young people can not only learn about different existing theories, but can text theories based on their own experiences and contexts. (Esther Ojulari, previously partnerships and programmes officer for ChildHope UK)

Principles of participatory training, sharing and immersion have been advocated through participatory learning and action processes over the years. Children and young people's participation needs a dual approach in encouraging flexibility and 'relaxed' use of participatory approaches and methodologies (Chambers, 2011) while ensuring there is a safe and participatory space for the engagement of children and young people with each other, and in dialogue with adults and decision-makers in communities. The debates in the early 2000s about the juxtaposition of child participation or protection, safety and ethics have more recently been seen as going hand in hand with participation by many national organisations, INGOs, donors and academic researchers. Many organisations working in participatory ways with children and young people have developed child protection policies and procedures to deal with issues of abuse and disclosure. Applying ethical protocols is an important aspect of rights-based research (Beazley and Ennew, 2006).

Conclusions: children at the centre of change

In order to achieve meaningful children and young people's participation, their evidence needs to be taken seriously and recognised by

DOI: 10.1057/9781137379702.0015

decision-makers including local adults in their families and communities. In turn decision-makers need to be convinced that children and young people can contribute to improving services and interventions intended to improve children's futures. In order to translate the rhetoric of rights into practice in a broad range of contexts as discussed in the 'Change-scape' presented in this chapter, participatory processes can seek to support strong mechanisms or strategies of communication and collaboration, creating participatory spaces and addressing local power dynamics, both within and outside organisational settings. Processes of capacity-building and identifying 'champions for children' can help to sustain interest, enthusiasm and belief in children and young people's capabilities.

In terms of progressing to systematically include generation and age analysis into the children's participation agenda, the following lessons are drawn from the interviews with children, researchers and managers in Nepal and the United Kingdom. Children's participation can lead to lasting positive changes in their lives and circumstances, and can avoid unintended negative consequences. Children can be both participants and/or facilitators of participatory planning and evaluation and, given responsive and child or youth friendly support such as mentoring, they can become more empowered as the process progresses. The involvement of other stakeholders in the participatory process should be encouraged from an early stage and continued throughout the process as confidence in children's participation amongst adults grows, thus shifting local adult-child and institutional power relationships as a key to lasting change. 'Gradually the awareness is growing in the global community about the valuable input that children can make and people can no longer deny the importance of their participation' (researcher from Nepal). These mechanisms have been reinforced and added by applying the Change-scape theory in training in Ethiopia, Peru and Sierra Leone. The following additional learning has been applied during these processes. Firstly, that in creating spaces for dialogue between community adults and children, children and young people still need separate spaces in order to build their confidence and to interact with decision-makers. Local adult women also need to be included, otherwise decision-makers in the community may only be identified as men and important gender power dynamics will be missed. Boys, girls, young men and women may need to work separately as well as together to bring out different issues that may affect their lives. Issues of difference such as dis/ability,

DOI: 10.1057/9781137379702.0015

ethnicity and religion also need to be considered in children's identity and inclusion in participatory processes. Child clubs that may be created in ongoing participatory action in communities need to continue to take power dynamics between children and with adults into account. This will take resources and time in order to achieve lasting change. Organisations will also have to review policies to support children and young people's participation. As capacity is built and staff and decision-makers become aware of the value of children and young people's input and of their capability and innovative ideas, trust in their evidence and roles in participatory processes can grow.

Note

1   Footage of the young woman refereed to can be found in the bottom left video clip at http://www.dvigc.com/open-space/.

DOI: 10.1057/9781137379702.0015

11

Essential Ingredients in Child- and Young-Person-Led Research

Cath Larkins and Young Researchers

▶ **Abstract:** *This chapter gives the young researchers' views on the three models for reflecting on participatory research that are presented in the chapters by Kerawalla, Michail and Hughes. The different strengths of each model are identified and suggestions are made for how these might appeal to different young people. The young researchers then identify eight key ingredients in child-led research: think about research as made up of lots of different stages; think about different influence in each stage; provide support for young people's leadership; adapt methods to suit the needs of individual children or young people; build trust; value difference but work towards agreements; adults should back off; and everyone should try to make it fun!*

Joanne Westwood, Cath Larkins, Dan Moxon, Yasmin Perry and Nigel Thomas. *Participation, Citizenship and Intergenerational Relations in Children and Young People's Lives: Children and Adults in Conversation.* Basingstoke: Palgrave Macmillan. DOI: 10.1057/9781137379702.0016.

This chapter is written by Cath Larkins and 'UCan' (a group of young researchers who have been working with The Centre for Children and Young People's Participation since 2012). The young researchers are Zac, David, William, Azraa, Ellie, Daniel, Reece and Rosie. We started working together as the Steering Group for a research project funded by the Office of the Children's Commissioner. We investigated the impact of low income on the rights of disabled children (see Larkins et al., 2013, Appendix 1 for details).[1] We are disabled young people who stand up for the rights of other disabled young people. When we started that project we were aged 12–18. We are all now a year older and the youngest group member has left.

How did we write this chapter?

Cath wrote two summaries of each chapter. One summary was two pages long. The other was half a page. Cath gave the summaries to the group and asked us to think about:

1   Whether we agreed with what each author said was important.
2   What else we thought was important for child-led research to work well.

We read the summaries, tried out the models different authors had proposed and then wrote down our opinions. Cath then wrote these ideas up as a draft chapter. We looked at the draft chapter, made changes and Cath wrote down these ideas and our answers. Cath put all of this together (with some extra ideas in boxes) and then some of us made final suggestions to complete this final version.[2]

What is in the next three chapters?

The next three chapters are about children and young people doing research. Lucinda Kerawalla (Cindy) has drawn a model for how to think about groups of young people doing research as a form of community action. Her chapter shows how she has developed this model from an earlier one that was used to think about how individual children do their own research/ learning project in schools. Reese, Ellie and Will think that Cindy's diagram is a good way of showing what happens in a group research project. It

DOI: 10.1057/9781137379702.0016

describes something very much like what we did. We think young people can use this idea and make it their own by drawing a bubble picture of their own research experience. When we did this, we each came up with slightly different stages in our research, but there were links between these stages, just like in Cindy's drawing. This might show how different parts of the process are more memorable for different children and young people.

Samia Michail's chapter explains that when you are doing child-led research, it is important for adults and young people to get to know each other, to have informal times together and to let young people opt out when we want to. To do this, adults should not always focus on the project. And adults need to think about children and young people as individuals and work out what support each person needs. Samia says this is difficult because it takes time, people are busy and it costs money. Rosie and Zac really agreed with Samia. They think building relationships builds confidence, which helps young people talk and share ideas. Rosie feels she talks more openly now, both in the research process and personal relationships (with family and friends), as a result of being involved in our research steering group. Zac feels that building relationships gives you the reassurance that you can speak to each other without feeling that what you are saying is stupid.

Martin Hughes's chapter provides a tool with which children and young people can evaluate their involvement as young researchers. He used a Q-Sort model (a way of ranking cards with different statements on them). By comparing the ways different young researchers ranked the statements on these cards, he has identified three different sorts of patterns in the ways in which young people see their involvement in research. Dan and David tried out part of Martin's method and thought that trying the method out is a really good way of understanding how it works. Using the statements Martin provided and thinking about their involvement in our steering group, Dan and David were able to show that they both strongly agreed that they were 'not bothered about having equal power relationships with adults in the research – they just wanted to be able to have a say'. They also agreed that they had not taken any 'responsibility for sorting out the ethical issues in the research'. They shared similar views, agreeing that 'changes to the research process were made as a result of what they had said' and that they were 'involved at the data analysis stage'. However, they had substantially different views about whether they 'needed adults to make sure that the project stayed on track' and whether, for them, this experience was 'a different way of

DOI: 10.1057/9781137379702.0016

adults and young people learning together'. Dan reflected that Martin's method shows the diverse ideas people have at certain times and he rather enjoyed doing the exercise.

What does all of this tell us about the key ingredients of group research with children and young people?

We think there are eight key ingredients in child-led research. To decide what these key ingredients are, we thought about these three chapters and our own experience.

Thinking about Cindy's model, provides a good way of thinking about how groups do research, because it helps you reflect and plan different stages of research. This made us think that the first key ingredient in group research with children and young people is:

1   Think about research as made up of lots of different stages

These are the stages of child-led research that we remembered taking part in:

▶ Meet
▶ Talk about why we are here and get to know each other
▶ Agree to take part
▶ Plan what to do at the next meeting
▶ Do introductions at meetings when new people are there
▶ Talk about different children's rights
▶ Look at case studies and different stories
▶ Act out our own stories
▶ Do drawings to tell stories
▶ Analyse films (of what has been found out so far)
▶ Plan research questions
▶ Meet with groups and individuals and put our research questions to them
▶ Feedback findings to group
▶ Discuss different stories from real life
▶ Think about the things that are right/good and what is wrong about what we find out
▶ Tell other people about what you are starting to find out
▶ Say what you think about the responses and how you feel about them

DOI: 10.1057/9781137379702.0016

▶ Reflect on the findings and your feelings
▶ Have ideas about how to share what you have found out (We decided to do a film. Cath had to do a report and we helped with this too)
▶ Make the film
▶ Show the film to our parents
▶ Show the film at Parliament to your MP, talk to the children's commissioner and maybe talk to people from TV and radio

Some things we do more than once and research can go around in circles at times, like in Cindy's model. Researchers do not have to do all of these things.

In our research, Cath and other adult researchers did the two stages written in italics, but they could have been done by young people. Also in our research different young people had influence over different stages. For example, Ellie gave a lot of ideas about which rights were important, Zac did the first draft of the questionnaire and Will had the idea of doing a film.

Our second key ingredient then is:

2 Think about different young people having different influence in different stages of research, according to their own choices and interests

We think this is important to think about because not all young people want to do everything that is involved in a research processes. This way of doing research follows the point Samia made in her chapter. She said that young people should opt in and out of research group activities, depending on what is going on in their lives and what interests them.

Learning from Samia's model, and the differences between the support Dan and David described needing in our research, we suggest a third key ingredient:

3 Give individual children and young people the support they need so that they can engage in and lead research in the ways they want to

As Samia has pointed out, this takes time and money, but it also requires building relationships. Through relationship adults get to know the young people they are working with, their ways of working and their preferences for support and levels of engagement. At the same time, young people build up relationships with each other.

This made us think of two more key ingredients:

4   Adapt methods and provide different activities for different young people within a group

Looking at the different research stages we took part in (listed earlier), and thinking about the different chapters we reviewed, it is really clear that different activities suit different young people. Some of us enjoyed Samia's drawing whereas others preferred Martin's cards and numbers. So, offer a group of children and young people a range of different activities.

It is useful to try models like those in the following chapters, but also support children and young people to adapt these to suit their own circumstances and preferences. In this way, rather than just having to following other people's ideas, children and young people can create new ideas. We can take idea from existing models for planning, doing and evaluating research to create our own.

As well as in the next three chapters, other examples of methods and activities that can be adapted by children and young people can be found on the website.[3]

5   Build trust

To make these sorts of research processes work, we feel trust is really important, for all children and young people. Trust starts with building relationships, like Samia talks about in her chapter. Then, when you trust others you feel more independent and you can put forth your own views. You have that trust in others that they will respect you, what you think and what is important to you. If you do not trust a person, you do not have that reassurance. Trust also involves following guidelines about consent and information (see website for our suggestions on this). We think trust also develops where you have time to deal with and find solutions to personal problems. There need to be times where adults listen to this and help you work out what you can do to sort out these difficulties.

Building trust also helps a sixth essential key ingredient to happen:

6   Value differences in opinion but work towards agreements

Group research needs to create spaces for recording and valuing differences in opinions between group members. And through this young people in the research group value and learn from the views of other young people who are less directly involved. Group-based research also needs to provide spaces in which common understandings and agreements can develop. We managed this in our research in the following manner:

▸ We wrote rules for our own group (but we felt this was a bit formal – we could have just talked about basic rules like 'Listen and don't shout').

▸ We had debates, where we listened to everyone's views and everyone had a chance to speak. Sometimes this took a long time, so that everyone felt comfortable to speak in front of the whole group.

▸ We supported different young people in the group having different roles.

▸ We voted (by throwing toys) to make difficult decisions about priorities.

To make all of this happen we had to have respectful conversations between young people, between adult facilitators and between adults and children, where everyone listed to each other and made compromises.

Once young researchers have built up experience and trust in each other, themselves and the facilitators, it is time for another key ingredient:

7 Adults should back off

Some young people can take a lead from the very first meeting. In our group, Zac led some activities on the first night, because he'd had experience of this sort of thing from the youth council. But all young people bring in their own ideas from other places and experiences. Hence it is important to give space for these ideas, so that we can put our previous knowledge into practice and come up with new ideas of things to do. Young people can run their own meetings. Adults should give guidance but not be bossy.

8 Make it fun

If you want young people to stay involved, you have to make the research fun. Adults should not be strict. You should play games. We did a lot of throwing teddies. It is also fun when we are in charge. For example, Zac was in charge of the music when we played Pass the Parcel (this was a

DOI: 10.1057/9781137379702.0016

research activity – the parcel had questions in). Zac loved being in charge because it meant he won something! It is also fun when you learn about new things, make friends with people and become more confident. We thought it is also fun to understand research more, and now be more able to lead the next project from the very start!

Notes

1   The group is facilitated by Cath Larkins, Lisa Carroll, Hans Mundry and Naomi Burgess. Cath co-directs The Centre. Lisa is a volunteer, who used to be a UCLan student. Hans works for Lancashire Young People's Service. Naomi works for Barnardos, Lancashire.

2   Details can be found at http://www.dvigc.com/book/cypresearchers/.

3   http://www.dvigc.com/young-people-conference/.

DOI: 10.1057/9781137379702.0016

12

Empowered Participation through Inclusive Inquiry

Lucinda Kerawalla

Abstract: *This chapter offers a multidisciplinary perspective on addressing the question: what is it about a young person's engagement with the research process that can empower them to participate in their community? The inquiry learning literature is drawn upon to resource the development of an inclusive inquiry framework that represents what the researcher needs to do in terms of research process, plus it describes how a young person can actively transform their position in their local community, from being a relatively powerless individual, to being an empowered advocate of community opinion. The example of a group of Girl Guides, working towards an award that requires them to carry out a community-based research project, is drawn upon to illustrate the process of self-empowerment through inclusive inquiry.*

Joanne Westwood, Cath Larkins, Dan Moxon, Yasmin Perry and Nigel Thomas. *Participation, Citizenship and Intergenerational Relations in Children and Young People's Lives: Children and Adults in Conversation.* Basingstoke: Palgrave Macmillan. DOI: 10.1057/9781137379702.0017.

Introduction

> Nobody empowers anyone ... *Although adults cannot empower children and young people, what they can do is promote and facilitate experiential learning processes through which children and young people can empower themselves.*
>
> (Shier et al., 2012, pp. 11–12; italics in original)

Imagine you are 12 years old again and after school you go to a local youth group where you take part in fun activities and regularly spend some time supporting the community by helping to maintain your local church. As part of the group's activities, you are working towards an achievement award for which you need to carry out some research into an issue relevant to you and your community. You and your friends think that the choice of local shops is limited, so you decide to investigate the opinions of local residents. You create a research question and decide to ask local people to complete a questionnaire. Once you have collected and analysed your data, you and your friends make a poster and discuss your achievements with the mayor of your town. A few weeks later, you carry out an inquiry into microclimates in the grounds of your school as part of your geography lessons. You work with a group of friends to develop a research question and then go outside and use some specialised equipment to measure air temperature, wind speed and humidity in various places. Back in the classroom, you analyse your data and write a short individual report which will be assessed by your teacher.

Both of these scenarios describe real events that took place during two different research projects in which I have been involved. Both projects involved young people in learning about and conducting their own research but the underpinning philosophy of each project was very different: children and young peoples' right to community participation through inquiry in the former and school-based learning through inquiry in the latter. But what do we know about *how* learning and/ or community participation can come about through engagement in inquiry? The educational, inquiry learning literature is extensive and has been concerned with increasing our understanding of inquiry learning processes (e.g., Klein, 1995; Chinn and Malhotra, 2002; de Jong, 2006; Littleton et al., 2012). However, there appears to have been little consideration in the sociological literature (which focuses on children's right to participate) towards elucidating *how* children and young people can become empowered citizens (i.e., be in a position to contribute to the

DOI: 10.1057/9781137379702.0017

local community on an equal footing to adults) by carrying out inquiry in their communities. Shier et al. (2012, p. 1) suggest that, where children and young people manage to make an impact on policy, 'we often know little about how it was achieved and how it might be reproduced'. The current chapter begins to address this shortfall by exploring the potential for cross-fertilisation between work which has focused on supporting children-and-young-people-as-researchers by educationalists and those concerned with the promotion of children's and young people's rights.

The question that arises is this: what is it about a young person's engagement with the inquiry process that empowers them to participate in their community? Synergies between the aforementioned bodies of literature are considered and an 'inclusive inquiry' framework is offered as a conceptualisation of how empowered participation through inquiry can be achieved and replicated. Empowered participation, in the current context, can be defined as being in a position to contribute to local decision-making by having empirical evidence of community support to back up your arguments. As an illustrative example of how the framework might be applied in practice, the community-based research carried out by a unit of Girl Guides is discussed.

Conceptual framework

The following conceptual framework is offered, based on the integration of the two aforementioned approaches to children and young people as researchers: children's rights and inquiry learning.

Children's rights

In recent years there has been a shift in Western understandings about the place of children and young people in society, which has been influenced in part by the United Nations Convention on the Rights of the Child (United Nations, 1989; UNICEF, 1995) along with the development of a new sociology of childhood in the 1990s (James and Prout, 1990/1997). Consequently, during the last two decades there has been a reconceptu-alisation of childhood where children and young people are recognised as human beings in their own right, as opposed to being incompetent adults-in-waiting. This new focus has led to a greater awareness of the right of children to carry out their own research into matters which affect them, and to provide evidence which can support arguments for

DOI: 10.1057/9781137379702.0017

potential change (e.g., West, 2004). Contexts where work of this nature has taken place include schools (e.g., Nash and Roberts, 2009; Fielding and Bragg, 2003; Cox and Robinson-Pant, 2008), communities (e.g., John, 2003) and care settings (e.g., Kellett, 2011b). This field has also produced manuals and guidelines for adults interested in supporting young peoples' research (e.g., Kirby, 1999; Kellett, 2005a; National Youth Agency, 2010; FLARE, 2009; Bucknell, 2012).

A substantial body of literature exists which identifies some of the tensions inherent in implementing this approach to facilitating young people's participation, such as the complexities of adult-child power relations (e.g., Bragg, 2007) and the problematic notion of 'voice' (e.g., Fielding, 2004; Cruddas, 2007; Thomson and Gunter, 2007). However, there remains the question of how a young person's engagement with the research *process* can lead to their empowered participation. What do young researchers *do* to empower themselves and how might adults facilitate this process? The educational inquiry learning literature can shed some light here.

Inquiry Learning

Inquiry learning has a long history (Dewey, 1933; Bruner, 1961) and can be described as being an approach that involves 'a process of exploring the natural or material world that leads to asking questions, making discoveries, and rigorously testing those discoveries in the search for new understanding' (National Science Foundation, 2000). Inquiry learning can take place in a wide variety of settings (e.g., schools, museums and at home) but most published work has focused on classroom-based inquiry learning contextualised within curriculum frameworks (Jones et al., 2012). There is a wealth of evaluation studies that make a compelling case for the effectiveness of inquiry learning in subjects as diverse as biology, physics and geography (e.g., Klein, 1995; Chinn and Malhotra, 2002; de Jong, 2006; Littleton et al., 2012; Kerawalla et al., 2011).

To date, the 'children's rights' and 'inquiry learning' approaches to children and young people as researchers appear to have remained separate by virtue of their different underpinning philosophies, and articles seem to be published mainly in either sociological or educational/psychological journals. However, there is one overarching similarity which unifies work in both fields: in order to be successful in conducting their own

DOI: 10.1057/9781137379702.0017

research, children and young people learn about the research process and how to operationalise it in terms of research activities. The educational, inquiry learning literature has offered various representations of the research *process* which describe it variously in terms of a cycle, spiral or series of steps (e.g., 'create a research question' or 'collect data') (for a more in depth discussion, see Scanlon et al., 2011). These steps specify *what* a researcher needs to do. They do not, however, attempt to represent the *relationship* the researcher has with the research process in terms of what/who they are researching. More recently, a 'personal inquiry framework' (Scanlon et al., 2011) was developed which goes some way to address this shortcoming (Figure 12.1).

The personal inquiry framework represents the research process in terms of eight iterative, interdependent phases which, importantly, are labelled in terms which acknowledge the researcher's relationship with what/who they are researching. The framework represents the personal relevance of a research topic (e.g., find *my* topic), the personal research choices that a researcher makes (e.g., decide *my* inquiry question or hypothesis) and the personal responsibility which a researcher necessarily commits to in order to complete their research project (e.g., plan *my* methods, collect *my* evidence).

The personal inquiry framework was developed to support school-based inquiries where the focus is on maximising the extent to which the young person owns, and is responsible for, the research process and

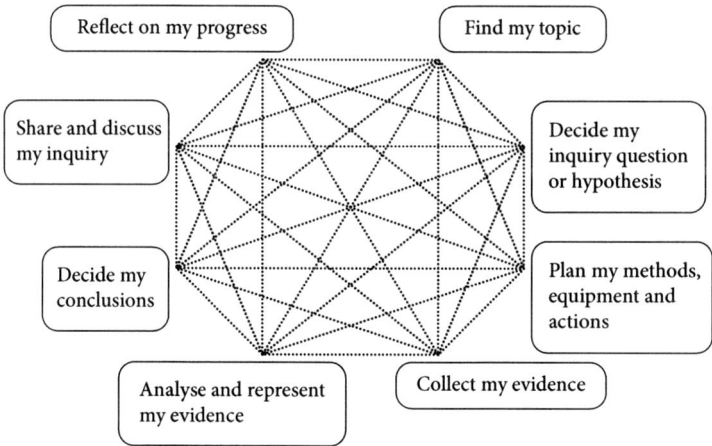

FIGURE 12.1   *The personal inquiry framework (Scanlon et al., 2011)*

DOI: 10.1057/9781137379702.0017

the end product (within institutional constraints such as equipment availability). The notion of *personal* inquiry was conceived not only to maximise opportunities for the learner to become engaged through making their own choices but also to encourage young people to reflect upon the consequences of their own actions on the world (e.g., in terms of personal behaviours which might impact on climate change). This focus on the *individual* (me) is consistent with an institutional agenda which values the testing and grading of work produced by individual pupils. As such, the framework has proved invaluable for representing and supporting the process of a range of school-based personal inquiries (e.g., Littleton et al., 2012; Kerawalla et al., 2011; Kerawalla et al., 2012; Anastopoulou et al., 2012).

An issue of interest to this chapter is whether or not the personal inquiry framework can be a useful tool for representing inquiries outside of formal educational contexts. Previous work suggests that it can be used to support the inquiry activities undertaken by young people attending an after-school club (Jones et al., 2012) – a hybrid environment in which the school agenda is present to some degree but where young people can continue their work at home. However, there remains the question of whether the framework is useful for representing the *participatory* nature of community-based research where there is no formal educational agenda. The following section discusses this question further in the light of some research carried out by a unit of Girl Guides (an international youth organisation for girls aged 10–14).

Research as a Girl Guide: Streets Ahead

Recently, I worked with a unit of Girl Guides to develop a new Go For It! badge (an achievement award) – Streets Ahead – that can be earned by Guides completing their own community-based research.[1] As I had worked previously with colleagues on the Personal Inquiry project that developed the school-based personal inquiry framework depicted in Figure 12.1, I was interested in exploring the extent to which the framework could a) support my development of the research activities that the Guides would need to undertake towards their badge (i.e., *what* they needed to do), and b) capture the participatory nature of the community-based work undertaken by the Guides (i.e., their *relationship* with what/who they were researching).

DOI: 10.1057/9781137379702.0017

The Streets Ahead badge activities: what needs to be done?

The personal inquiry framework was effective in identifying the essential phases of the research process, as represented by each point on the octagon in Figure 12.1. Each phase could then be populated with associated research activities and resources which could be adjusted to fit the timeframes available. A range of both pre-existing and tailor-made activities were undertaken by the Guides during each phase of their research. For example, Kellett's (2005a) 'think sheet' was used by the Guides to support their identification of a topic and the creation of their research question. Questionnaire development was resourced in several ways using tailor-made resources: firstly the Guides completed simple questionnaires themselves, to familiarise them with both five-point Likert scale (e.g., I enjoy Guides – strongly agree, agree, neither agree nor disagree, disagree, strongly disagree) and yes/no/don't know (e.g., do you like the Guide uniform?) item formats, and to help them to understand the difference in granularity between the response types. They then drafted their own questionnaire items and copied the final versions onto a blank questionnaire template which was later photocopied and distributed to participants for completion. Analysis was resourced with tally sheets and the Guides were encouraged to reflect on their data collection by completing a simple questionnaire (e.g., What went well? What would I do differently next time?).

It can be concluded that the personal inquiry framework proved to be a valuable tool for resourcing the process of the Guides' research in terms of identifying the phases of their research – *what* needed to be done. Also, it represented the iterative nature of inquiry, such as when research questions were refined. However, it was less successful at representing the *participatory* nature of the Guides' research, which is addressed in the following section.

Community research as inclusive

One of the key differences between the school-based research described in the introduction to this chapter and the research carried out by the Guides is the extent to which the young people were acting as individuals. During the school-based research, the young people worked in

DOI: 10.1057/9781137379702.0017

groups but the overarching focus was on the learner as an individual; they produced individual reports which were assessed. However, the role of the Guides as individuals underwent some important changes as their research progressed. The Guides worked in small groups and identified a topic to research which they found interesting and relevant to their lives. One of the groups chose to focus on the shops in their local town and their work will be presented as an exemplar for the purposes of this chapter. The group identified a joint concern that the variety of shops in their town was not as broad as it could be; at this stage the focus was very much on the Guides as individuals (we *each* think there should be more variety of shops). However, the Guides' relationship with what and who they had decided to research changed with the creation of their research question, which was: 'do *we* need new and better shops in *our* town?' (my italics). So, what began as a topic of interest to each individual group member was rapidly transformed into an investigation into community opinion – do members of *my community* agree with *me*? The research question identifies each Guide as a member of their community and the focus of the research effectively shifted from 'me' to 'us'.

The group then created a questionnaire which consisted of the following items requiring a yes/no/don't know response (the names of the town and its shops have been anonymised):

1   Do you ever shop in Greenfields?
2   Do you like shopping in Greenfields?
3   Do you go into more than three of the shops?
4   Do you shop in the charity shops?
5   Would you like more varietys (sic) of shops?
6   Do we need a clothing shop?
7   Should we have an [entertainment] arcade?
8   Should we only have a Food shop?
9   Do you like the idea of the new Big supermarket in Greenfields?
10 Are you going to use the new Big supermarket?

By asking members of the community to respond to these questions, the Guides had opened up their initial, personally relevant topic to community opinion. In this sense, their research was no longer just about 'me'. By canvassing local opinion, and analysing the questionnaire responses provided by community members, the role of the Guides became one of 'me working for us'. Moreover, when the Guides presented their findings (posters) to their local mayor (Figure 12.2), they were speaking as

DOI: 10.1057/9781137379702.0017

FIGURE 12.2   *Empowered participation (Guides presenting their work to their Mayor)*

community *participants* who, by virtue of the evidence they had generated, had empowered themselves to advocate for community opinion.

An inclusive inquiry framework

The transformations in the Guides' relationship with what and who they were researching do not appear to be represented in the personal inquiry framework. Figure 12.3 proposes an 'inclusive inquiry' framework which goes some way to address this issue.

The inclusive inquiry framework (Figure 12.3) maintains the integrity of the research process described in Figure 12.1 but each inquiry phase has been relabelled in terms which describe the relationship between the researcher and their community. For example, 'collect my evidence' has been replaced with 'record community opinion'. Data is now described in more subjective terms; it belongs to, and represents, the community in which it was generated. Data analysis and the creation of bar charts (e.g.) is therefore more a process of 'analysing and representing community opinion'. It follows, therefore, that instead of 'sharing and

DOI: 10.1057/9781137379702.0017

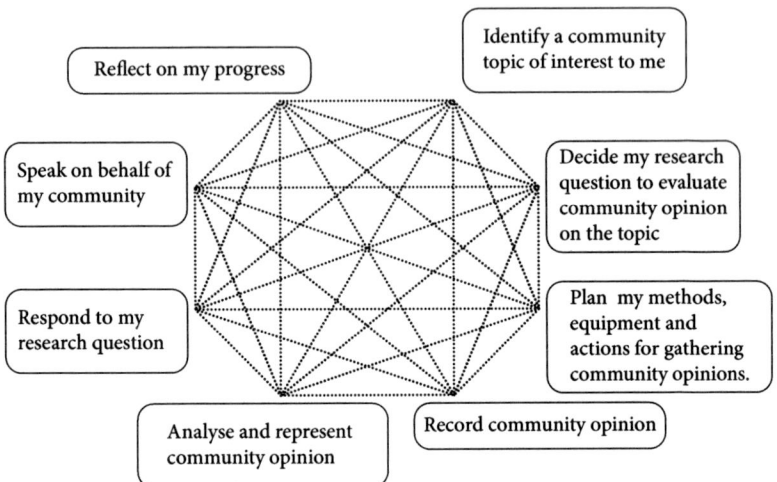

FIGURE 12.3   *The inclusive inquiry framework (adapted from Scanlon, Anastopoulou, Kerawalla and Mulholland et al., 2011)*

discussing my inquiry' by talking to the mayor, the Guides were instead 'speaking on behalf of my community'. The focus here is very different to the school pupils discussed earlier who were carrying out an investigation so that they could write an individual report for assessment by their teacher.

The inclusive inquiry framework therefore represents how a young person can become an advocate for community opinion by engaging in each phase of the inquiry process. The benefits of the inclusive inquiry framework are twofold: it represents *what* the researcher needs to do in terms of their engagement with specific phases of the research process, plus it simultaneously describes how a young person (or anyone else) can actively transform their position in their local community, from being a relatively powerless individual, to being an empowered advocate of community opinion. The focus is less on 'me' and more on 'me working for us'. The researcher is then in the position to canvas for change and build arguments based on empirical data. On this occasion, the Guides were satisfied with the award of their Streets Ahead badge and did not want to pursue any changes in policy or practice, but this does not preclude other young people doing so in the future.

DOI: 10.1057/9781137379702.0017

Conclusions

This chapter has identified the synergies between the children's rights perspective and the educational approach to children and young people as researchers and has offered a new inclusive inquiry framework as a representation of how children and young people can become empowered participants in their communities through inquiry. Importantly, the Guides were not empowered by their Guide Leader or by the adult researcher, they empowered themselves through their engagement in the research process and their participation in various research activities (see Shier et al., 2012). The Guides' activities were supported by adults: the Guides, for example, learnt new skills and were given parental assistance with distributing questionnaires to members of their local community. Throughout, the adults were facilitators who worked with the Guides in developing their understandings of the research processes and the tools which they could harness to empower them to carry out their own research and to participate as citizens in their neighbourhoods.

The 'inclusive' inquiry framework renders visible the contributions made by various adults, so the Guides' research takes on a distinctly dialogic nature. Their work was essentially co-constructed and necessarily represented a cacophony of voices. The multivoiced nature of the Guides' research suggests that it would be beneficial in future to explore how children and young people use the resources produced by adults to mediate their own work, and how they might design their own resources for use by children and young people in the future.

Note

1 See http://www.girlguiding.org.uk/guides/gfibadge/gfi/streetsahead.html.

DOI: 10.1057/9781137379702.0017

13

Re-crafting Child-Led Research for Australian Welfare Services: The 'How' of Working alongside Children

Samia Michail

▶

Abstract: *In 2011, UnitingCare Burnside implemented a Child-Led Research (CLR) program, for the first time in Australia producing positive outcomes for children. The program delivered an inimitable means in which to teach children 'how' to create their own knowledge and facilitated their contributions to their own emotional and social well-being. This is a critical reflection on the CLR program, re-crafted for children living in disadvantaged communities. It explores 'how' they achieved through the genuine hearing and responding to the whole child – not just their voices. It discusses time and relationships as key elements for research and practice, raising questions about the potential of CLR within the welfare sector.*

Joanne Westwood, Cath Larkins, Dan Moxon, Yasmin Perry and Nigel Thomas. *Participation, Citizenship and Intergenerational Relations in Children and Young People's Lives: Children and Adults in Conversation.* Basingstoke: Palgrave Macmillan. DOI: 10.1057/9781137379702.0018.

DOI: 10.1057/9781137379702.0018

Introduction

The shift to children and young people being involved in research has enjoyed a period of uncritical enthusiasm, but there is growing demand for more reflective questioning on the complex philosophical, political and methodological issues that have arisen (Loveridge, 2010). Until recently, the literature on children and young people's participation and hearing their voices has largely neglected critical appraisal of what it is that motivates children and young people to genuinely engage with adults in research or with the research itself.

There are now multiple and complex ways in which children and young people engage in research, but this chapter is interested in the shift to children leading their own research, and specifically within the context of children and young people's service provision. Child-led research (CLR) has been implemented in many contexts around the world. One of these contexts has been a non-governmental organisation (NGO) that has children and young people's well-being as its core business. This specific program has led to an opportunity to reflect on '*how*' to do CLR, but also on the consequences of this approach. In this chapter we contemplate the mechanics of CLR and examine relationships among children, young people and adults, as a key element of working alongside them. We also explore the role and impact of these relationships, using a specific case of children and young people leading research. This will help us to extend on the readily available advice to adults on building rapport with children and young people and apply it to research environments.

We begin this chapter by briefly considering the concept of relationships, and the specific UnitingCare Burnside (Burnside) CLR program. The second section presents arguments on ways in which relationships are critical to working alongside children and young people when they lead research. The third section takes a brief look at the consequences of implementing CLR and what it teaches researchers about their practice. We conclude by inviting practitioners and researchers to reflect on relationship as a key tool in research with and by children and young people.

What do we know?

The fundamental importance of building positive relationships between children and adults can be traced back to Bowlby's (1953) exploration of

DOI: 10.1057/9781137379702.0018

secure attachments and the work of Ainsworth and Blehar (1978) on the links between attachment and behaviour. Over time, we have come to recognise exactly how fundamental child-adult relationships are to children's well-being. Relationships are defined here as distinct from interactions with children and young people. They are the *way* we connect with each other, usually involving emotion.

We know that in early childhood, child-adult relationships enhance children's sense of well-being and social competence and influence children's happiness (McAuley and Layte, 2012, p. 541; Holder and Coleman, 2009). In Australia, recently introduced early childhood policy highlights that quality care involves developing relationships that are 'responsive, respectful and promote children's sense of security and belonging' (Council of Australian Governments, 2009, p. 25). Child-adult relationships are pivotal for achieving positive outcomes in children's learning (Michail, 2011; Burton, 2006) and are intertwined with student behaviour (McCluskey et al., 2008). Social work is carried out within a network of human relationships and it is the connection built between worker and client that is the key feature of therapeutic work. However, the significance of relationship within social work is often undervalued (De Boer and Coady, 2007, p. 40). This researcher would add that it is not valued in most research processes.

Child-adult relationships are especially fundamental to research where children and young people are involved, as potential subjects and active participants in research (Christensen and Prout, 2002), and now as researchers in their own right. Children's participation is a relational process involving emotion and power (Prout and Tisdall, 2006). Hence, a focus on the relational processes among children, young people and adults is persistently being welcomed as the way to understand child-adult relationships (Uprichard, 2010; Mayall, 2002b). However, a more nuanced understanding of, and detailed discussion on, the nature of child-adult relationships in research is needed (Jupp Kina, 2012), to better understand how they are formed and the impact they have on children and young people, researchers and generating of knowledge.

Child-led research at UnitingCare

In 2011, Burnside implemented a CLR program for the first time in Australia. It contained two parts; teaching children and young people the research process and supporting them to complete their own research project. Burnside staff recruited nine children and young people aged between 10 and 13 years,[1] who were receiving a Burnside service. They had diverse experiences, including repeated exclusion from school, living in poverty, learning disabilities and living in foster care. Many of the children and young people were experiencing one or more of these social issues at the time of the program. These experiences provided some of them with capacities beyond their years and for others their circumstances had stinted their development.

The programme began in April 2011 as an adaptation of Kellett's (2005b) 'club' style of delivery.[2] It was adapted significantly to meet the range of challenges pertinent to both the status of children and young people and the risks of living in communities of disadvantage. Children and young people are at risk of marginalisation when they have limited opportunities to express themselves or extend their skills (Michail, 2013). The programme responded to concerns about CLR only being offered to privileged children and young people (those with access to educational opportunities and supports), and went beyond being interested in the views of children and young people merely because they are service users, as raised by Brownlie (2009, p. 702).

The 'how': relationship

A key element of the programme – the building of relationships – is essential in explaining the 'how' of working alongside children and young people as they genuinely engage. Many observations of the CLR program suggest that whether children and young people become engaged in the research process is based on the ability of the child-adult relationship to capture their focus. Often in research there is limited capacity to build comprehensive rapport. Authors often write about the 'research relationship'. At times this implies a clinical set of interactions that is time-limited and derived from children and young people only for the purposes of the research. Connections with children and young people in CLR were fundamentally distinct and did not specifically seek to ensure quality data or rigorous research outcomes (although this did occur). Connections were primarily about increasing children and young people's competence in research and deliberately designed as a process within CLR that required

DOI: 10.1057/9781137379702.0018

researchers to relate to children and young people on an individual, personal level.

Christensen and Prout (2002, p. 484) reaffirm that research relationships always take place within social relations. We were cognisant that 'the ability of the facilitator of a participatory process to relate to the participants fundamentally impacts on their willingness to participate fully in the process' (Jupp Kina, 2012, p. 207). These distinct connections required us, as adult facilitators, to give of our personal selves. We began our programme by getting to know each other personally using structured tasks and informal time spent together. We drew self-profiles, talked about each other's personalities, articulated people's strengths and shared our hopes for the future. We maintained these reciprocal connections as part of the program.

Nonetheless, there were times when individual children and young people chose not to connect with adults by not engaging in the programme. For example, they selected when to be attentive to adults, or to not participate in suggested activities and/or not contribute to discussions. In so doing, the child or young person did not respond to the efforts of others or actively work to build the child-adult relationship. Children and young people could be pre-occupied with peer relations or their own thoughts. When they made the choice to disengage from adults, we observed that this impacted on their capacity to continue with their research work in an adequately focused way. They were less able to absorb the content of the session and the progress they made on their projects was limited.

Our programme was designed to be child-led, and therefore we were able to account for the meaning of children and young people's silences (Lewis, 2010) by respecting their decisions to not engage. However, we also needed to balance the process of research with research outcomes. We made the program timetable flexible to accommodate informal times with the children and young people and re-connect with them. Some children and young people did not finalise their research but presented on their experience of participating in the research process. For these children and young people, the process of building relationships helped them reflect beyond their project to their research learning and personal gains in terms of skills and well-being. These gains were not measured by adult metrics but in the children and young people's reflections to evaluators[3] (Newell et al., 2011).

Adults also contributed with different intensity at different times. Relationships are a two-way street and there is a need to review

DOI: 10.1057/9781137379702.0018

the personal impact we have on children and young people in the research space (Jupp Kina, 2012, p. 202). When adults applied more of their efforts into the content of the session, overlooking the needs of individual children and young people, and their personal relationship with them, research became a set of tasks which the children, young people and adults found difficult. The importance of these observations lies in recognising the rare ability of our programme model to prioritise relationships with children and young people. It allowed researchers, child or young person and adult, to work alongside each other and address individual need. Our awareness of adult contributions to relationship in research also indicates the need for reflexive practice that can increase researchers' self-awareness of the way they shape research.

Time

Building relationships with children and young people takes time (Alderson, 2008, p. 287; Punch, 2004, p. 99). Spending time interacting, listening and establishing dialogue was essential in CLR for people to build connections with each other. Repeated and sustained positive exchanges with and between children and young people enable them to demonstrate a renewed commitment each time they meet. Creating a programme that delivers these exchanges over an extended period of time shows how the child or young person is valued.

Conversely, the common time constraints that exist in research are a significant barrier to solid relationships. These constraints can come from children and young people themselves who are busy people (Kellett, 2011a, p. 208), but they can also come from structural inequalities within research funding systems (Lewis, 2010). CLR is a resource-intensive programme largely due to adult time. Yet, adult time translates into solid supportive relationships, flexibility in program delivery and the capacity to respond to children and young people's needs. The translation occurs as the adult researcher is consistently available, which demonstrates their personal, ongoing commitment to the child/young person's growth in the understanding of research. It is the long-term and intensive nature of CLR that makes it successful (Newell et al., 2011). Adult time provides opportunities for children and young people's meaningful contribution to knowledge of the world.

DOI: 10.1057/9781137379702.0018

Despite this understanding, real anxieties exist about funding programmes that work with small numbers of children and young people for extended periods of time. There is particular reluctance around practices that produce long-term, intangible outcomes that are difficult to measure. There is even greater resistance to (and no established system for) funding children and young people's research, undoubtedly linked to qualms about rigour and validity. In response, we note the mounting quality of research from children and young people (see http://www.childrenyoungpeopleandfamilies.org.au/research/child-led-research and www.dvgic.com for examples) that has been produced. Misgivings about the potential of children and young people generating knowledge are related to our traditional expectations around who should produce knowledge, and in what form it must be presented, to be considered rigorous and valid. Overcoming these requires a shift away from long-standing conceptualisations of children and young people as incompetent and lacking agency.

The consequences of CLR: roles and responsibilities

There has been much discussion about the different roles that adult researchers can play in research with children and young people (see Christensen and James, 2008, p. 229). They are important roles and often change based on factors such as the stage of research, individual characteristics and context. Children and young people also take on these varied roles that range from leading to learning. In CLR, many children and young people completed surveys or interviews for each other, debriefed together, encouraged or discouraged their peers' presentation skills. Some mediated a difference in opinion or shared strategies they found successful for addressing their difficult situations.

Thinking about the roles of children and young people and adults in a prescribed way may restrict our understanding of the fluid and flexible nature of child-adult relations. In reality, the roles that children, young people and adults take on, in respectful child-adult relations, change incessantly. More interestingly, when working with children and young people who are researchers, these roles require ongoing negotiation. Our experience is that the researcher role was pertinent to children and young people only during CLR sessions and more specifically at different points of a session or stage in their research project. At times, they wanted to lead

DOI: 10.1057/9781137379702.0018

specific activities. At other times, they directed adults or other children and young people to lead. The activities used in a session were planned by adults but were often 'overtaken' by children and young people, modified, adapted and used in ways that they found more interesting.

In the CLR program there was ebb and flow in the way children and young people took on the responsibilities of research. By way of example, two children presented their findings at an Australian conference, being described as child researchers. They took on this researcher persona, standing quietly, reading over their notes. They engaged with the adult audience and their responses were positive, respectful and thoughtful. They showed interest through their willingness to answer questions. Directly preceding and after their presentation, they were rowdy, talking about other topics and fidgety. As one child was being transported back to her home, her demeanour changed notably and on enquiry she explained, 'I'm just Kathy[4] again'. As adults, we are keen to bestow upon children and young people the title of researcher in recognition of their capacity to generate expert knowledge about themselves and knowledge of the world. However, they are yet to become comfortable in these roles and to find a place for them in the routine of their everyday lives. Supportive relationships can encourage an individual to become objectively aware and step outside themselves. Children and young people may benefit from solid relationships within which they can negotiate these newly formed research roles that bring both rewarding and challenging experiences.

The challenge: context, needs and temporality in CLR

The nuances articulated here about the fluidity of the child-adult relationship have arisen from deliberation about the successes and failures of our CLR programme. It is not sufficient for us as reflexive researchers to just claim that good relationships and lots of time lead to successful programmes. Reflexivity in research is important (Punch, 2002) and fundamental to understanding *how* we use relationship over time to build spaces for children and young people to lead (De Boer and Coady, 2007).

Working with children and young people as researchers results in new complexities and uncertainties in the research process because they introduce to us new social relations in the field (Christensen and Prout, 2002). Considering these new dynamics, it is important to respond to

DOI: 10.1057/9781137379702.0018

the new potential of relationships that is conducive to engagement. A multi-dimensional lens in our reflection reveals three key areas: context of the relationship, the needs of the child within that contextual relationship and the issues to do with time (the duration and timing) of that connection with respect to the child's life.

Context

Christensen and Prout (2002, p. 483) tell us that establishing dialogue with children and young people makes it possible to better understand the social relations that they are part of. However, immersing oneself into a social relation, becoming part of it, gives direct experience of that social relation. In so doing, we begin to understand the social relation but also increase in social competency. The research tasks we completed together in the Burnside CLR programme (e.g., playing card games) functioned not only as the mediums for communication, but as the basis of our relations with children and young people, so increasing their competency.

Fattore et al. (2007) further assert that 'activities are the contexts in which children experience and negotiate competencies and relationships'. This is also true of shared activities in the family context (McAuley et al., 2012, p. 449). CLR teaches children and young people about social competences because they are required to lead others (children, young people and adults). They therefore must engage with the research relationship more deeply, more personally, than if they did not own the research. There is a reciprocity which is difficult to ignore. One child summarised his social learning in this way: '[A]fter coming to here, it sort of taught me a lesson. Socialise with other people and not with computers or technology, because they can't talk back to you, whereas people can [sic]'.

Needs

It is vital that the needs of the child within the contextual relationship are dictated by the child. Children and young people are experts on their own lives (Mason and Danby, 2011) and when they conduct research are often more determined to overcome their disadvantages (Alderson, 2008, p. 287). Moreover, when a child feels safe in a relationship, this

DOI: 10.1057/9781137379702.0018

promotes self-awareness and increases the likelihood that they can articulate their needs. For example, one child-led the decision to present her research by writing a story. This child had previously experienced a dearth of opportunity to express her views on her care arrangements. She was delighted to be able to verbally tell her story through research. For this child, her need was to be publicly heard (quite literally), and it was met when adults supported the dissemination of her research findings in a way that was personally meaningful.

Temporality

Children and young people's needs within the same context change over time. They require varied support depending on their circumstances, and in CLR, they led us to respond to those circumstances. It is tempting to provide a barrage of instructions or encouraging comments to a child or young person when what is needed is the reassurance that someone is willing to work alongside them. For example, one child negotiated that he would be more at ease speaking to a large audience if he were able to turn side-on and look at me while presenting. On arriving at the lectern, we confirmed our pre-determined strategy. To my surprise, as he began to speak, he turned to face the large audience. His needs had changed within a few minutes. I was now needed in a different way and therefore stood behind him silently throughout his presentation.

We need to remember that children and young people's relationships are dynamic (Greig et al., 2007, p. 49), as is their participation, and the degree to which they engage changes constantly (Howarth et al., 2012). We thus need to peer through a multi-dimensional lens, repeatedly and frequently, to reflect on our work with children and young people.

Conclusion

The significance of child-adult relationships to children and young people in any context, including research, is irrefutable. This may be common practice for some practitioners and researchers, but what is absent is the dialogue about the place and function of these relationships in practice and research. These detailed conversations are important to the progress of children and young people's capacity to generate

DOI: 10.1057/9781137379702.0018

their own knowledge. The comprehensive accounts provided from the Burnside CLR programme demonstrate that there is much to be learnt from the way we utilise relationships with children and young people. The accounts presented here do raise serious questions about the capacity of the existing welfare and research systems to truly work alongside children and young people in the individual, intensive and tailored way which has been shown to genuinely engage them. However, they have also shown that child-adult relationships provide a common mechanism by which practitioners and academics in research can communicate on the best way to encourage children and young people's participation. The challenge to be met is how to use the understanding of relationship to reconfigure systems that constrain the accessibility, effectiveness and utilisation of CLR.

Bessell (2009) draws our attention to the distinctions between method and methodology. In a similar vein, we contrast the difference between simply affirming that we 'should' build positive relationships with children and young people and practicing 'conscious, critical reflection of types of relationships available to us in our work with children' which 'affords us an opportunity to reconstruct relationships which are mutually life-enhancing and liberating' (Sorin and Galloway, 2006, p. 20).

Notes

1   We note that it is important to think critically about the role of age in assessing children and young people's needs. Our experience was that age-based assumptions about children and young people's capacity was not a particularly useful tool in determining what children need with respect to skill, knowledge or support within a research context. This was an incredibly important aspect of working with children and young people from disadvantaged communities.

2   Children and young people met for two hours per week over an 18-week period. We planned additional research time during school holidays with built-in recreational activities.

3   CLR was independently evaluated by the NSW Commission for Children and Young People and the Centre for Children and Young People at Southern Cross University. For the full evaluation report, see http://www.childrenyoungpeopleandfamilies.org.au/__data/assets/pdf_file/0009/86859/Child-LedResearchAPilotoftheToday_and_TomorrowResearchProgram.pdf.

4   Pseudonyms have been used to maintain confidentiality of CLR participants.

DOI: 10.1057/9781137379702.0018

14
What Might Adults Learn from Working with Young Researchers?

Martin Hughes

▶ Abstract: *This chapter explores young people's viewpoints concerning their experience of working on a research project with an adult. Some of the reasons for involving young people as researchers are discussed and a brief description of Q Methodology is given before describing how it was used to explore the viewpoints of young researchers in this study. The viewpoints arising out of the analysis of the young people's Q sorts are described. Conclusions drawn from the study are discussed before then returning to two key themes concerning empowerment and epistemology. Some of the implications of these findings are indicated in addition to some pointers to work that has followed the completion of the study.*

Joanne Westwood, Cath Larkins, Dan Moxon, Yasmin Perry and Nigel Thomas. *Participation, Citizenship and Intergenerational Relations in Children and Young People's Lives: Children and Adults in Conversation.* Basingstoke: Palgrave Macmillan. DOI: 10.1057/9781137379702.0019.

> When we ask children to participate as 'researchers' rather than as the objects of classroom investigations, what is the character of this social identity we ask children to take on? Warren (2000, p. 123)

Introduction

The study reported in this chapter began with my interest in exploring the effective engagement of professionals with 'hard to reach' children and young people (Hughes, 2007). In a project designed to explore the experiences of young people described as having 'emotional and behavioural difficulties', I enlisted the help of young people as 'co-researchers'. My interest in their position grew and my work with them led to my problematising the term 'co-researcher', developing into my concern to understand the experience of young people who are thus engaged. Much is written concerning the involvement of young people as researchers, indicating a prevalent view that it is a 'good thing'. This chapter explores young people's viewpoints concerning their experience of working on a research project with an adult and what such activity might achieve.

I start by contextualising this study within participation, young people's voice and their subject position, as there are a number of overlaps with the growing literature on young researchers, a discussion of which then follows. Consideration is given to the way in which young people are positioned and the methodological position that I adopted, which sets the scene for reporting the viewpoints of young researchers using Q Methodology. Issues related to empowerment and research quality are discussed before briefly considering if the involvement of young people as researchers leads to their empowerment or results in better research. Other themes are discussed in relation to the literature (power, voice and relationships) and implications for young researchers, participation and practice are explored, along with some pointers to work that has followed in the wake of the study.

Why involve young people as researchers?

Participation

Participation forms an important contextual backdrop for young people as researchers, as young people are often doing research activities that

DOI: 10.1057/9781137379702.0019

FIGURE 14.1   *A continuum for participation*

have been initiated or suggested by adults and go on to complete them *with* adults or at least where adults adopt some kind of role in the activity. Participation can mean a range of types of engagement. At a simple level, the continuum above (Figure 14.1), drawing on the work of Sinclair (2004), captures some of this diversity.

Whilst there appears to be a strong theme in the literature that participation is 'positive', this is an over-simplification. Indeed, if 'the biggest ethical challenge for researchers working with children … is the disparities in power and status between adults and children' (Morrow and Richards, 1996, p. 98), then one might be tempted to conclude instead that young people have a voice when adults allow them to. The benefits of participation are also questioned by researchers such as Percy-Smith (2005, 2007) who, critical of the limited impact that participation has had on young people's lives, points to target-driven policies which often fail to reflect the actual lives that young people lead, *their* concerns and priorities, and inflexible adult-led bureaucracies which struggle to facilitate young people's participation. Nonetheless, Prilleltensky et al. (2001) make links between power and control, health and wellness which thus manifests strong justification for encouraging young people's participation, where greater involvement is more likely to lead to improved psychological health.

Voice

The nature of children's voices in child-led research is a second area of concern. Ravet (2007a) describes the shift in voice research from information-gathering and regarding children as objects to a focus on empowerment with children as subjects. James (2007, p. 262) argues that 'giving voice to children is not simply or only about letting children speak' but also about children's perspectives helping us to better understand the social world. She discusses the rhetoric about 'giving voice to children' and problems related to authenticity (translation, interpretation and mediation), the use to which voice is put, a glossing over of

DOI: 10.1057/9781137379702.0019

multivocality and the nature of young people's participation in research, including as 'co-researchers'.

The subject position of children and young people in research

> Young people ... are typically positioned as both dependent, vulnerable receivers of care and education, and sometimes 'agentic' subjects with distinct voices'. (Komulainen, 2007, p. 13)

Children and young people are frequently described in terms that contain contradictions. On the one hand, adults see them with agency, and on the other, as inadequate and underdeveloped. They have needs and deficits compared with the adults that they are to become (Burman, 2008) but also rights and competencies (James et al., 1998).

As opposed to viewing them as becoming adults, Punch (2003) favours an approach which takes children's views seriously, focusing on their being rather than their becoming. Uprichard (2008) avoids homogenising and reducing the complexity of childhood by considering two discourses together, regarding children as *both* being *and* becoming.

Young researchers

As the literature on young researchers has grown, the extent of participation and voice has been debated. 'The 1990s witnessed the development of new ways of working with children within the new social studies of childhood, repositioning children's voices at the centre of the research process' (Barker and Weller, 2003, p. 35). For more than a decade there has been a developing interest in research projects which involve adults and young people working together which Brownlie et al. (2006) describe as 'reflected in a linguistic shift from talking about "research on" to research with' and now, increasingly, to "research by" children and young people' (Brownlie et al., 2006, p. 6). For many this theme is located within 'Participation' and has a strong emancipatory intent. However, inevitably, there are a range of views on this matter, with Birbeck and Drummond (2007, p. 22), for instance, claiming that the principle outlined in Article 12 'has not greatly influenced research pertaining to children' and that 'research with children tends to be a process that is devised by adults, applied to children with results interpreted by adults, generalised and presented as a theory of childhood'.

DOI: 10.1057/9781137379702.0019

Worrall and Naylor (2004, p. 1) found that '[t]he majority of students saw the process of being selected and trained to carry out research as a positive experience and emphasised their delight at being chosen to carry out such a demanding task'. Clacherty and Kistner (2001) make a case for participatory research as a therapeutic process.

Much of the literature concerning work with young researchers draws on the UNCRC (1989) as a rights-based model. Young people have a right to research issues which are of concern to them and so, in turn, a right to be helped by adults to achieve this. Grover (2004, p. 90) claims that the status of children as individuals with rights is enhanced when they are allowed to be active participants in the research process and 'heard in their authentic voice'. Grover stresses the need for young people to speak from their own perspective as collaborators so that young people can tell the stories of their lived experiences, which strengthens the research process and increases its relevance.

Pointing to a number of conceptions of children's subject position in research, Davis (2009, p. 156) offers a number of reasons for involving children in research:

▸ Pedagogical benefits (children learn from the experience)
▸ Political potential (opportunity to change social policy and exercise rights)
▸ Epistemological (improved understanding and better research)
▸ Children as consumers (better services result)
▸ Protectionist (respectful dialogue promotes child protection)

A number of writers stress ways in which involving young people as researchers can be beneficial to the research. Young people can identify research questions and issues that adult researchers might miss, help to clarify the language used for their peers, enable adult researchers to gain greater insight into youth issues, learn new research skills and remain aware of the perspectives of young people (Kirby, 2004). Young people may be able to obtain relevant data from their peers, more easily than adults can (Flores, 2008; Kellett, 2010; Kirby, 2004), facilitated by closer intimacy and greater understanding between the researched and the researcher (Alderson, 2001). Mahon et al. (1996) suggest that young researchers are less likely to be perceived as experts, although whether or not they are more or less likely to receive 'public' or acceptable accounts as a result is unclear.

Bishop notes that 'it is rare that projects include the step of asking participants to evaluate the actual process of the research that they

DOI: 10.1057/9781137379702.0019

participated in' (Australian Research Alliance for Children and Youth and New South Wales Commission for Children and Young People (2008, p. 28). Brownlie (2009) echoes a number of writers when she comments that little has been published on the perspectives of young researchers, so that knowledge about the benefits of young people's participation in research is related to the projections of adults rather than being rooted in children and young people's experiences.

Thus, as reported in relevant literature, the reasons for encouraging the participation of young people overlap with features related to involving them as researchers. We find rhetoric surrounding this topic, but few attempts to understand the views of young people who have worked as young researchers.

Understanding the viewpoints of young researchers using Q Methodology

Methodological considerations

So as to explore the viewpoints of young people concerning *their* experiences of working as researchers, I was keen to seek a methodological approach that enabled me to hear a range of voices, reduce complex data and illuminate something of significance related to what being a young researcher means. Q Methodology gives voice to all participants (including the marginalised) and remains close to the experiences of the disempowered (Brown, 2006). I wished to avoid imposing the researcher's view of the world on the people being researched, respecting participant's viewpoints.

I wanted a focus that saw children and young people as diverse individuals with unique experiences, capable negotiators of reality, who construct different realities and live within multiple realities, able to weave stories to create order out of chaos and make sense of their world moment by moment. I attempted to create a 'climate of perturbation', instead of pursuing 'psychology's "wild goose chase" after nomothetic knowledge' (Stainton Rogers, 1997). If I was serious about voice, then I needed to explore and understand approaches that facilitate co-construction between researcher and researched. Q Methodology seemed a good choice, serving as an example of what Ravet (2007b) refers to as an ethical methodology.

DOI: 10.1057/9781137379702.0019

Q Methodology

Q Methodology is a method designed to capture the subjective or 'first-person' viewpoints of a single participant or, more usually, a group of participants. A *Q-set* is created, consisting (often) of a set of statements, all of which relate to the topic being investigated. Participants are asked to then express the extent to which they agree or disagree with each of these statements, by placing them on a grid (called a *Q Sort*[1]).

A Q-set typically consists of between 40 and 80 statements/items (Watts and Stenner, 2005; Stenner et al., 2008). I developed a set of 59 which reflected the perspectives of the young people I was working with and the themes found in the literature.[2] Statements in this research were designed to complete this lead phrase: *In my experience, young people working with adults on research...*

By working with young 'co-researchers' on a 'real' project I immersed myself in the communication surrounding this topic through regular visits, conversations, being open to 'co-researchers' observations and comments, and critical reflection. The Q-set statements initially came directly from young people themselves and include:

▸ Are given the opportunity to take on additional responsibility
▸ Is a good way to get a different view on the chosen subjects
▸ May not fully understand what is going on
▸ Are accepted as an equal, valid member of the team
▸ May feel under pressure to complete
▸ Enable me to see how more experienced people work
▸ Have a lot of responsibility
▸ Have to plan very carefully
▸ Are valuable in offering and sharing new ideas
▸ Have to share ideas together

Key ideas in the literature were also transformed into one or more statements. For instance, 'the biggest ethical challenge for researchers working with children is the disparities in power and status between adults and children' (Morrow and Richards, 1996, p. 98), led to these statements:

Experienced frustration over the limits which were placed on them by the adults
Found that power-sharing (or democracy) between adults and young people in research was possible

DOI: 10.1057/9781137379702.0019

Found that it was clear that the adults felt that they knew best
Found that adults were willing to adopt a learner role

These statements relate to responsibility and decision-making:

Took responsibility for sorting out the ethical issues in the research
Were much more than just assistants to the adults
Made some really important decisions

Whilst these were examples of statements related to outcomes:

Experienced a different way of adults and young people learning
together
Helped to produce better outcomes than work produced by adults alone
Were able to learn how more experienced people work

The basic method then involves three stages: (1) the gathering data on the participants' views in the form of Q sorts; (2) the inter-correlation and factor analysis of those Q sorts; (3) the interpretation of the emergent main viewpoints participants held in common.

Participants in the study were recruited by asking the young people I was working directly with as 'co-researchers' to participate in my research and contacting other young people engaged in research. I also contacted adults who had a view about young researchers because they had either written about them or worked with them, or both. However, this chapter shows the results from the young people only.

There were 34 young researchers in this study, ranging in age from 13 to 23[3] some of whom I met, others with whom I corresponded, sending the Q sort materials by post or email.

Having collected Q sorts from participants, the data were entered into PQMethod (Schmolck, 2001) to analyse Q sort data and to extract and rotate factors so that they could then be interpreted. Factor extraction involves 'the identification of distinct regularities or "patterns of similarity" in the Q sort configurations' (Watts and Stenner, 2012, p. 139).

Results

The analysis revealed that there was enough similarity between the Q sorts to indicate that there were five distinct patterns (factors) or viewpoints and the young people's individual Q sorts that were most closely associated with each of them.[4]

DOI: 10.1057/9781137379702.0019

To illustrate this briefly, here are examples of the five statements that were most agreed and most disagreed with for three of the viewpoints I focus on in this chapter:

Statements most agreed with (including the numbers these statements were given for analysis purposes):

Viewpoint 1

In my experience, young people working with adults on research...

▸ were trusted by adults (16)
▸ were respected as an equal, valid member of the team (42)
▸ were much more than just assistants to the adults (3)
▸ had a lot of responsibility (43)
▸ enjoyed their involvement with the project (57)

Viewpoint 2

▸ felt included in the process (52)
▸ got on well with the adults (59)
▸ needed the adults to make sure that the project stayed on track (9)
▸ took responsibility for data collection (13)
▸ were trusted by adults (16)

Viewpoint 5

▸ were much more than just assistants to the adults (3)
▸ contributed to research which was just as good as research done by adults only (29)
▸ experienced a different way of adults and young people learning together (27)
▸ had an equal but different contribution to make to the research process (33)
▸ felt that they were kept in the loop (55)

Statements (and reference numbers) that were most disagreed with:

Viewpoint 1

▸ felt that their involvement was tokenistic (e.g., superficial, insignificant, unimportant) (20)
▸ found that it was clear that the adults felt that they knew best (47)
▸ needed the adults to make sure that the project stayed on track (9)
▸ felt under pressure to complete the project (41)
▸ needed support from adults in order to keep taking part (49)

Viewpoint 2

> ‣ experienced frustration over the limits which were placed on them by the adults (4)
> ‣ came up with the idea for research (25)
> ‣ had a say in how money involved with the project was to be used (11)
> ‣ felt that their involvement was tokenistic (e.g., superficial, insignificant, unimportant) (20)
> ‣ got involved for the good of the community (58)

Viewpoint 3

> ‣ felt that their involvement was tokenistic (e.g., superficial, insignificant, unimportant) (20)
> ‣ found that it was clear that the adults felt that they knew best (47)
> ‣ experienced frustration over the limits which were placed on them by the adults (4)
> ‣ had a say in how money involved with the project was to be used (11)
> ‣ felt under pressure to complete the project (41)

Whilst it is of use to understand which items were agreed and disagreed with by each of the viewpoints, this is not the whole story; and the reader should note that the interpretations given here are based on a reading of the *entire* pattern of each of the factors, based on the factor arrays (of the idealised Q sort for each factor). In this way, positions in each of the factor arrays are compared so that the level of agreement is relative rather than absolute. One is looking for items in a factor array that have been placed with greater or less agreement, in contrast to where items have been placed in the other factors.[5]

Analysis

So as to interpret each viewpoint, the array of statements was arranged to create a single Q sort exemplifying the viewpoint and these were in turn analysed qualitatively.

Space has not permitted detailed discussion of viewpoints 3 and 4. However one brief point to note is that whereas the three young people's viewpoints discussed here had some similarities to the adult viewpoints, 3 and 4 were related to each other, but unrelated to the adults' views, in that they both share a sense of distance from adults.

DOI: 10.1057/9781137379702.0019

Viewpoint 3 was named *Was it worth it? Worked hard, took the flak, gave the research status, doubted the outcome.* These young people did a lot of work on the project, did not enjoy their (more tokenistic) involvement as much as young people with other viewpoints as in addition to the work and hassle that they dealt with, they felt less included, under pressure to complete, did not understand what was going on or get on particularly well with the adults.

In contrast, Viewpoint 4 was named *Easy life! Bit of power, not much responsibility, a bit of a laugh.* Young people with this viewpoint came up with the idea for the research and had some power without too much responsibility. They had limited opportunities to express their views about the research and were little more than assistants, compared with other viewpoints, less trusted, less respected and needing adult support.

The young people's Viewpoints 1, 2 and 5 can be summarised as follows.

> Viewpoint 1: Powerful team players – responsible, trusted, team members, keen to have and develop greater power.

Young people came up with the research idea. They were better at getting responses from other young people but were not sure that they knew enough to be researchers. They had little influence over how research was used and did not see that it led to things changing. They were regarded as equal team members, valued for offering new ideas and listened to when they did so. *Young people had responsibility and did not need adults to keep them going. They were keen to have power.*

> Viewpoint 2: Happy assistants – happy to assist adults in their work.

Young people were not initially drawn to the research for the opportunity to work on issues important to them or their community and had very limited influence and decision-making. More than the other viewpoints, they had a *narrowly defined area of responsibility that the adults were clear about, almost in the role of assistants to the adults who needed to support their continued participation in the project. They did not experience frustration about this position and felt included.* The results that they contributed to were taken seriously and they saw a final report.

> Viewpoint 5: Equal partners-experts who gained a sense of power-sharing with adults.

Young people had limited decision-making opportunities. They were regarded as experts and did not feel that their involvement was tokenistic,

DOI: 10.1057/9781137379702.0019

where adults knew best. They were much more than assistants to the adults and at times, it seems that adults had an assistant role. Their contribution led to research that was just as good and publishable as that produced by adults working alone, although they were not involved with feeding results back at the dissemination stage. *The project gave them a sense that power-sharing between adults and young people was possible and they experienced a different way of learning with adults.*

Discussion

Through this work, I have supplanted the term 'co-researchers' with 'young researchers' which avoids some of the assumptions related to power and equality (i.e., that adult and young researchers share equal status). We find that with five young people's and three adult viewpoints, there is not a 'one-size-fits-all' solution. The situation is more complex than being able to conclude that young researchers are a 'good thing'.

Bucknell (2012) states perhaps an ideal position when she writes that, in one study, '[t]he young researchers...were unanimous in confirming choice of topic as a crucial motivational factor', whereas the 'actual' experience of several young researchers (as found in their completed Q sorts), shown by the placing of statement 25, indicates, again, greater variation.

We can consider two of the reasons for involving young people as researchers, given by Davis earlier, namely, political potential (and empowerment) and epistemological (better research) by looking at how some of the statements cluster together and contrast across the young people's viewpoints. For instance, YPF1 and YPF5 share some similarities in relation to power:

Item number and content wording	YPF1	YPF2	YPF5
Needed support from adults in order to keep taking part	Disagree	Neither	Disagree
Weren't bothered about having equal power with adults in the research – they just wanted to be able to have a say	Disagree	Neither	Disagree
Were consulted about all of the key decisions	Agree	Disagree	Agree

FIGURE 14.2   *Item number and content wording (1)*

DOI: 10.1057/9781137379702.0019

Viewpoint 2 also indicates that in contrast to viewpoints 1 and 5, they tended not to make really important decisions, including decisions about how research findings were communicated (see statements 6 and 14). Whether or not the young people viewed that they contributed to better research (see statements, 2, 26 and 29) is hard to determine, as in this respect the viewpoints are 'mixed'. In other words, it is not clear from this research whether or not adults who work with young people can enable them to feel empowered *as well as* produce better research with the young people than adults working alone. However, *adults* in this study seem to regard working with young researchers as involving empowerment *or* research – not both.

To understand better what is required for young people to feel as though they are empowered, we can look at other items that set viewpoints 1 and 5 apart from viewpoint 2, thus providing some clues perhaps for adults and their 'researching behaviour' when working with young people as researchers. Positions in the factor arrays of each of the items are shown in brackets. Interestingly, getting on well with adults in a joint research project does not seem to be so important to feelings of empowerment for these two (YPF1 and YPF5) viewpoints.

Item number and content wording	YPF1	YPF2	YPF5
32 were regarded as the experts – they knew what young people were like	Agree (1)	Disagree (−2)	Agree (3)
46 were valuable in offering and sharing new ideas	Agree (3)	Disagree (−1)	Agree (1)
3 were much more than just assistants to the adults	Agree (4)	0	Agree (5)
9 needed the adults to make sure that the project stayed on track	Disagree (−4)	Agree (4)	Disagree (−3)
53 were protected from risks by the adults	Disagree (−2)	Agree (2)	Disagree (−1)
41 felt under pressure to complete the project	Stronger disagreement (−4)	Disagree (−2)	Stronger disagreement (−4)
47 found that it was clear that the adults felt that they knew best	Stronger disagreement (−5)	Disagree (−3)	Stronger disagreement (−5)
59 got on well with the adults	Weak agreement (1)	Strong agreement (5)	Weak agreement (1)

FIGURE 14.3 *Item number and content wording (2)*

DOI: 10.1057/9781137379702.0019

When young people are closer to the role of assistant, as the three viewpoints discussed here tended to disagree with item 4, we might reason that this does not appear to be a 'negative' experience for them. These findings suggests that Franks's (2011) concept of 'pockets of participation' can be useful. Envisaging young people's participation in research as a continuum may well incur criticism similar to that levelled at Hart so that working at the top levels is assumed to be 'better'. One way of countering this would be to examine the nature of the research activity, discuss with young people an appropriate role so that there is participative ownership of facets of the project 'so that participants become stakeholders in the research rather than owners of it in total'. This echoes comments by Davis (2009) who doubts that a single perfect way of involving children in research exists and rather than regarding participation as a 'moral imperative', 'it might be more helpful to see it as an approach that can be applied to research in many different ways, depending on the context'. Kirby (2004) also suggests that it is the situation that determines whether young people are involved all the way through or for a few stages only.

Item Number And Content Wording	YPF1	YPF2	YPF4
4 experienced frustration over the limits which were placed on them by the adults	−3	−5	−4

FIGURE 14.4   *Item number and content wording (3)*

During the early stages of my project I had approached the young people I was hoping to enlist as 'co-researchers' by explaining that I was seeking help with developing statements about behaviour. I had decided on my approach and methodology and although would have tried to include them had they been interested in the data collection and analysis, defined a 'pocket' for their participation. I was interested to learn therefore that of the nine participants significantly associated with viewpoint 2, six of the young people were connected to me, in that I had worked directly with them during the second round of the initial project. I was gratified that they had been happy to be the assistants that I was seeking.

DOI: 10.1057/9781137379702.0019

Closing comments

The results from this study indicate a number of different viewpoints held by young people, based on their experience of having worked as young researchers. Whilst some of the young people's viewpoints are focused on empowerment, it is unclear whether young people also believe that their contribution leads to better research. As epistemology is more of an adult concern, it is perhaps unsurprising that young people are not motivated to engage as young researchers for reasons similar to those given by adults, in all respects. The results hint at some adult behaviours that might be considered if projects aim to promote young people's empowerment, including regarding young people as more than assist-ants, trusting and not pressurising them to keep the project on track, utilising their knowledge of what young people 'are like', valuing ideas that they offer, not behaving as if 'adults know best' and enabling them to engage in some risk-taking. Adults need not, perhaps, worry too much about 'getting on well' with young people that they work with – perhaps good working relationships follow from the establishment of these other features.

Having concluded this study, I mused that research is like finding out, which is like learning. One adult participant (Jan) reported that *young people often say to us... if school had been like this I might have left with some qualifications*. How might this inform how we work with young people in places of learning, such as schools? James and James (2004) state that young people describe their ideal school as 'respectful' and also discuss the importance of others listening to what they say. Some young people seem to experience a different way of adults and young people learning together (statement 27) and we might translate other findings into a school context. For instance, there is some evidence from this study that young people might be encouraged to participate more, or be more empowered, if adults were to give them a sense that power-sharing (or democracy) between adults and young people in research is possible (24), that the knowledge that they bring with them is respected (32), that they have an equal but different contribution to make to the research process (33), that they are helped to understand what is going on (39) and that they feel that they are being kept in the loop (55).

DOI: 10.1057/9781137379702.0019

Notes

1 See http://www.dvigc.com/book/cypresearchers/hughes-annex/ for details of what this looks like.
2 http://www.dvigc.com/book/cypresearchers/hughes-annex/.
3 http://www.dvigc.com/book/cypresearchers/hughes-annex/.
4 http://www.dvigc.com/book/cypresearchers/hughes-annex/.
5 The Factor Q sort values for each statement were consulted for the analysis and are available on the website http://www.dvigc.com/book/cypresearchers/hughes-annex/.

DOI: 10.1057/9781137379702.0019

15

Conclusion: Moving Forward Participation, Citizenship and Intergenerational Relations – Ongoing Conversations and Action

Joanne Westwood, Cath Larkins, Dan Moxon, Yasmin Perry and Nigel Thomas

Abstract: *The closing chapter draws together the themes of participation, citizenship and intergenerational relations. The authors' contributions to developing effective practice are highlighted, together with a reflection on the process of facilitating children's and young people's participation in the writing and editing The chapter closes with a discussion of the key ways to achieve the participation of children and young people in research with them and about their concerns. Accountability, which is central to achieving children and young people's citizenship, and is a mechanism for moving towards intergenerational relations to enable children's participation rights to become a reality.*

Joanne Westwood, Cath Larkins, Dan Moxon, Yasmin Perry and Nigel Thomas. *Participation, Citizenship and Intergenerational Relations in Children and Young People's Lives: Children and Adults in Conversation.* Basingstoke: Palgrave Macmillan. DOI: 10.1057/9781137379702.0020.

Participatory research with young people is beginning to establish itself as a recognised form of research. However, behind each piece of research sit institutions and the networks that create them, pedagogies and epistemologies through which they are processed, and actors and powers that enable or curtail their access to the public arena. All of these factors frame the way in which research with children and young people takes place, and crucially influences the knowledge research creates and the impact it has. By involving young people in the conference, book editing and website, we have gone some way to bringing young people's voices into the aspects of research that are above and beyond involvement in a singular piece of research. Reflecting on this process our team and others involved identified many more opportunities in which we can create true collaborative conversations between the research community and children and young people. It was clear that the ICRYNet conference and Different Voices in Global Conversations is a first step in a longer journey, and there is much further work to be done. We have captured many examples of the dialogue between adults and children and young people on www.dvigc.com¹ and encourage readers of this book to access the materials available. Areas for development include promoting the views of children and young people from outside the developed West, working as much with children as we do with young people, and increasing the levels and amount of participation and collaboration between adults and young people across the board. In that sense it is important that Different Voices in Global Conversations be viewed as an emerging practice, one that is progressive with still some distance to travel. This not in the sense that new methodologies were developed for working with young people, indeed most of the techniques used had already been used in participation practice within the United Kingdom, but that these were applied to new communities of practice, institutions and sectors whose work influences the way in which we think about children and young people today.

   In this chapter we revisit the chapters of this book and consider how these conversations between children, young people and adults can take forward our understanding of the key themes of this book. We then point to some key ways forward.

Participation

There is a need to recognise the importance of multi-dimensionality when conceptualising participation. This was evidenced in the

DOI: 10.1057/9781137379702.0020

discussion in the chapter by Johnson who explores the application of the Change-scape model which was developed in response to the limits of purely listening in participatory work. The participatory model discussed earlier by Hatton requires adults to communicate and respond, sharing the potential that the participatory approach may not yield the results or outcomes children and young people expect or demand. In Kerawalla we saw how the combination of children's rights theory and inclusive enquiry methods enabled girls and young women to tackle community issues. As has been explored throughout this book participation in all of its dimensions needs to be developed and implemented with young people as co-creators. There are clear challenges in moving from words to action. We have seen several examples in this book of children and young people believing that their words alone do not have sufficient power to effect change. Embracing the multi-dimensionality of participation would also ensure that children and young people could decide which aspects of a participatory process they could get involved in and take control over. This suggestion was tested out and discussed in the chapter by Hughes and applied to formal settings and mechanisms in the chapter by Preston Youth Council and in an international comparison by Crowley.

What is clear from the contributions discussed here is that in the effective conceptualisation and application of participation there is a need for:

▸ children and young people to decide for themselves about their goals; and
▸ change to have an effect beyond the young people – in practice, policies and structures and in the (re)distribution of resources.

Citizenship

A key theme emerging from the discussion about the roles and tensions in children and young people's participation is in their status as citizens. In many of the examples of participatory and inclusion practice we have seen that children and young people have moved well beyond the traditional roles as consultees, into roles where they are involved in processes and in some cases protagonists where they are actively seeking ways to effect community-wide change. The type and level of support they

DOI: 10.1057/9781137379702.0020

require to be effective changes over time and adult participation workers need to respond to these changes.

Citizenship implies having a status which is deserving of respect amongst peers and the wider community and, in some cases discussed here, we have seen such advances in how children and young people have influenced and changed the way structures operate. Where children and young people are accepted as decision-makers and where democratic structures are available to promote this, a key mechanism of support lies in the level of accountability in the democratic systems. Despite the structural constrains on children and young people's access to resources and influence, they can still take action in their everyday lives and there are ways in which they can effect change. In the chapters by Jupp-Kina, Kerawalla, Nuggehalli and Lucas we saw how children and young people are disrupting accepted concepts of childhood and traditional constructions of child–parent and professional dynamics. The reciprocal learning and reflection which children and young people experience as co-researchers, as child language brokers and as community activists challenge dominant ideas of children as dependent and adults as providers. In many examples this book has illustrated the dimensions of citizenship which children and young people respond to and adopt.

▸ Citizenship and its relationship to participation implies acceptance that children and young people have rights to challenge adult-centric constructions of childhood and social justice.

▸ Participative structures have to be explicit about their ability and willingness to support children and young people's claims for citizenship by including mechanisms for making decision-makers responsive.

Intergenerational relations

The role of facilitation and adults and children and young people as facilitators was another key theme which emerged in this collection. As we have seen there is not a single process model or a one-size-fits-all approach. Instead the dynamics and successes of these activities rely on relationally between the actors, and a constant reflexive approach to unpacking the question of who has access to exercising power in any given moment. As we have seen in the discussions here there are

DOI: 10.1057/9781137379702.0020

approaches which empower or disempower children and young people, but a deeper critical exploration suggests that children and young people may wish to only engage in discrete elements of participatory activities. In Hughes's chapter, for example, some young people chose not to join in with all of the research activities and processes. That is their choice.

The dialogue between all parties and structures needs to be ongoing and relies on children, young people and adults' moving towards consensus about what is to be achieved. A model which incorporates the intergenerational dimensions, ongoing discussions on the same theme and a willingness by all parties to present their rationale and justification for movement and progress has to come from both sides. Adults have to be accountable when they refuse to move or take forward the ideas and demands of children and young people and this was noted specifically in the discussion by Johnson, Michail, Youthforia and in the debates over children, young people and their relationships with and access to space covered by Billett.

▸ A focus on the dynamics and potentials in intergenerational relations has the potential to co-construct the problems to be addressed as well as the methods and approaches which are needed to tackle them.
▸ Children and young people have to be given access to resources which enable them to decide how they will engage with adults and about what issues.

Ways forward (from young people and authors)

The chapters in this volume underline some of the challenges that have been identified in previous research where, as Crowley notes, young people's engagement in participatory processes has not resulted in change. Indeed we have seen examples of children's contribution as citizens through actions in their everyday lives, such as language brokering (Lucas) simply not recognised. These challenges leave us in a situation where 25 years after the introduction of the United Nations Convention on the Rights of the Child (UNCRC), the social positions of children and young people versus adults have not equalised. Children and young people as a social group remain excluded from most of the formal political and economic spaces in which decisions about the use of resources are taken and information

DOI: 10.1057/9781137379702.0020

about the appropriate rights and responsibilities of childhood are discussed and produced. But looking at changes in migration, family roles and economic opportunities reveals that children and young people are taking on increasing responsibilities; they are not in the traditional spaces or living the protected lives that dominant constructions of childhood would suggest. Some children have responsibilities that might be seen as equal to some adults: so why do we continue to propose diluted versions of participation which can still be all about talk and not about action? If adults do not allow innovation then children and young people will be constricted by how things have always been. If we carry on consulting, we are doing what others have done before us, adults asking, children talking, perhaps with some listening but no one taking enough action to bring about change.

Two strategies for addressing these challenges are suggested by authors in this volume. The first is recognising the potential of protagonism, where young people are supported to act directly as change makers in their own lives and in the lives of others, alongside at times asking others to help bring about change. The second is prospecting for and grasping opportunities and open doors that give access to people and structures that welcome being influenced by children and young people's views.

Opportunities for participation to result in the kind of citizenship that children and young people aspire to, require intergenerational relations to alter. These are some steps which may help that process of change:

▸ Pay greater attention to the role of facilitation, so that adults stand back from exercising power themselves.
▸ Accept and welcome new ideas and innovation.
▸ Draw decision-makers into existing participatory spaces, so that they have to engage in dialogue with children and young people.
▸ Avoid antagonism: train adults to shift their understanding of the local realities of children and young people's lives, give them experience and information about possibilities for participatory approaches from across the globe and then their capacity and trust in participatory processes will increase.
▸ Give children and young people information about successful examples of participation leading to change, so that they can learn from these models and adapt them to local situations.

Participation conceived of protagonism and grasping opportunities has transformational potential if it is followed as a fluid and dynamic

DOI: 10.1057/9781137379702.0020

process of change co-created by children and young people and their adult supporters. As long as children and young people are setting the agenda for change, then making the most of opportunities that arise to progress their agenda remains a child-led form of participation. This turns consultations on its head.

Accountability

One danger in focussing on pushing open doors is that children and young people may only then work with adults who are likely to respond positively to their demands, and these may not be the adults who have the power or resources to bring about the changes that young people seek. There is therefore a need to create new mechanisms through which adults and institutions can be held accountable for responding to children and young people's wishes. These should supplement and complement those formal structures which currently exist, but should be devised in partnership with children and young people and should draw on mechanisms which they have access to or where they can carve out pathways.

Policy changes and measures are subject to public scrutiny and accountability for economic viability and environmental impact. More recently assessments of the impact of policies on children's rights have been introduced in the United Kingdom and the European Union, whilst the UNCRC monitors children's rights and the way in which countries meet their duties and obligations and a UNCRC complaints mechanism is developing. Our recommendation drawn from the discussions in these chapters and at the conference is to orient such assessments towards participatory citizenly dialogue and to measure the extent to which there is meaningful and effective dialogue between children and young people, the organisations who work with them and for them and, crucially, policy-makers. In this way new policy measures or schemes would automatically need to evidence how they have sought out the dialogues and incorporated these into their plans and proposals. This would require policy-makers to embed the findings of many previous consultations and resist the temptation to call for new ones. Children and young people's organisations for the last 25 years have gathered enough evidence and recommendations to inform this orientation. Learning from the parallel conferences which sparked the

DOI: 10.1057/9781137379702.0020

idea for this book, there may also be opportunities that arise from using virtual and technological spaces to enable children and young people to cross the boundaries into excluded spaces, so that they can gain access to formal structures from their own homes. There are films and audio materials provided about participatory methods on www.dvigc.com[2] and we encourage readers to contribute to this web-based resource. We can learn more, alongside children and young people, about how to use these to better effect.

The remaining challenge is to facilitate action stemming from the ideas, concerns and challenges which have been discussed in this book, presented at the conference and which have been raised in other arenas focused on children's participation and citizenship across the globe. As these practices are replicated by more children and young people and the adults living and working alongside them, this will enable us to move from global conversations to global action.

Notes

1   http://www.dvigc.com/open-space/.
2   http://www.dvigc.com/talks/children-as-researchers/ and http://www.dvigc.com/workshop/young-people-and-research/.

DOI: 10.1057/9781137379702.0020

Bibliography

Agnew, J. A. (1987) *Place and Politics: The Geographical Mediation of State and Society.* Boston: Allen & Unwin.

Ainsworth, M. and Blehar, M. et al. (1978) *Patterns of Attachment: A Psychological Study of the Strange Situation.* Hillsdale, NJ: Erlbaum.

Alanen, L. (2009) 'Generational order'. In Jens Qvortrup, William A. Corsaro and Michael-Sebastian Honig (eds), *Handbook in Childhood Studies.* Houndsmill, Basingstoke: Palgrave Macmillan, pp. 159–174.

—— (2001) 'Explorations in generational analysis'. In L. Alanen and B. Mayall (eds), *Conceptualizing Child-Adult Relations.* London: Routledge-Falmer.

Alderson, P. (2010) 'Younger children's individual participation in "all matters affecting the child" '. In B. Percy-Smith and N. Thomas (eds), *A Handbook of Children and Young People's Participation: Perspectives from Theory and Practice.* London: Routledge.

—— (2008) 'Children as researchers: Participation rights and research methods'. In P. Christensen and A. Prout (eds), *Research with Children: Perspectives and Practices.* New York and London: Routledge.

—— (2001) 'Research by children'. *International Journal of Social Research Methodology*, 4(2): 139–153.

Anastopoulou, A., Sharples, M., Ainsworth, S., Crook, C., O'Malley, C. and Wright, M. (2012) 'Creating personal meaning through technology-supported science learning across formal and informal settings'. *International Journal of Science Education*, 34(2): 251–273.

Archer, D. and Cottingham, S. (1996) *The Reflect Mother Manual: A New Approach to Adult Literacy*. London: ActionAid.

Arnott, M. (2008) 'Public policy, governance and participation in the UK: a space for children?', *International Journal of Children's Rights*, 16(3): 355–367.

Australian Research Alliance for Children and Youth and New South Wales Commission for Children and Young People (2008) *Involving children and young people in research [electronic resource]: a compendium of papers and reflections from a think tank co-hosted by the Australian Research Alliance for Children and Youth and the NSW Commission for Children and Young People on 11 November 2008*. Accessed at http://www.aracy.org.au/cmsdocuments/REP_Involving_Children_and_Young_People_in_Research_2009.pdf.

Badham, B. (2004) 'Participation – for a change: disabled young people lead the way'. *Children and Society*, 18(2): 143–154.

Barker, J. & Weller, S. (2003) 'Is it fun?' Developing children centred methods'. *International Journal of Sociology and Social Policy*, 23(1/2): 33–58.

Bearne, E. and Marsh, J. (2007) 'Chapter 10, Uncomfortable spaces'. In E. Bearne and J. Marsh (eds), *Closing the Gap: Literacy and Social Inclusion*. Stoke on Trent: Trentham Books, pp. 133–140.

Beazley, H. and Ennew, J. (2006) 'Participatory methods and approaches: tackling the two tyrannies'. In V. Desai and R. B. Potter, *Doing Development Research*. London: Sage.

Beetham, D. (1994) *Defining and Measuring Democracy*. London: Sage.

Beresford, P. (2007) 'The role of service user research in generating knowledge-based health and social care: from conflict to contribution'. *Evidence and Policy*, 3(3): 329–341.

Bessell, S. (2009) Research with children: thinking about method and methodology *Involving Children in Research*. Sydney, ARACYand NSW Commission for Children.

Billett, P. (2012) 'Lessons from the field: Ethics in youth social capital research'. *Youth Studies Australia*, 31(3): 43–50.

——— (2011) 'Youth social capital: getting on and getting ahead in life', PhD thesis, University of Wollongong.

Birbeck, D. J. & Drummond, M. J. N. (2007) 'Research with young children: contemplating methods and ethics'. *Journal of Educational Enquiry*, 7(2): 21–31.

Blackledge,A. (2004) 'Constructions of identity in political discourse in multilingual Britain'. In, A. Pavlenko and A. Blackledge

DOI: 10.1057/9781137379702.0021

(eds), *Negotiation of Identities in Multilingual Contexts*. Clevedon: Multilingual Matters.

Bourdieu, P. (1986) 'The forms of capital'. In J. Richardson (ed.), *Handbook of Theory and Research for the Sociology of Education*. New York: Greenwood Press.

Bowlby, J. (1953) 'Some pathological processes set in train by early mother child separation'. *The British Journal of Psychiatry*, 99(415): 265–272.

Boylan, J. and Dalrymple, J. (2009) *Understanding Advocacy for Children and Young People*. Maidenhead: OUP and McGraw Hill Education.

Bragg, S. (2007) ' "Student voice" and governmentality: the production of enterprising subjects'. *Discourse: Studies in the Cultural Politics of Education*, 28(3): 343–358.

Bridge, G. and Watson, B. (2000) *A Companion to the City*. USA: Blackwell Publishing.

Bronfenbrenner, U. (1979) *The Ecology of Human Development: Experiments by Nature and Design*. US: President and Fellows of Harvard College.

Bronfenbrenner, U. (Ed.) (2005) *On Making Human Beings Human: Bioecological Perspectives on Human Development*. Thousand Oaks, CA: Sage.

Brown, S. (2006) 'A match made in heaven: a marginalized methodology for studying the marginalized'. *Quality and Quantity*, 40: 361–382.

Brownlie, J. (2009) 'Researching, not playing, in the public sphere'. *Sociology*, 43(4): 699–716.

Brownlie, J., Anderson, S. and Ormston, R. (2006) 'Children as researchers'. Edinburgh: Scottish Executive Social Research. Accessed at http://www.scotland.gov.uk/Publications/2006/06/SprChar.

Bruner J. S. (1961) 'The act of discovery'. *Harvard Educational Review*, 31(1): 21–32.

Bucknell, S. (2012) *Children as Researchers in Primary Schools: Choice, Voice and Participation*. London and NY: Routledge.

Buriel, R. (1998) *The Public Discourse on Bilingual Education: Myths and Realities from a Social Ecology Perspective*. Riverside: University of California.

Buriel, R., Love, J. De Ment, T. (2006) 'The relationship of language brokering to depression and parent-child bonding among Latino adolescents'. In M. Bornstein and I. Cote (eds), *Acculturation and*

Parent-Child Relationships: Measurement and Development. Lawrence
Erlbaum Associates. *Myths and Realities from a Social Ecology
Perspective.* Riverside: University of California.

Burman, E. (2008) *Deconstructing Developmental Psychology.* Second
edition. London: Routledge.

Burton, P. (2009) 'Conceptual, theoretical and practical issues in measuring
the benefits of public participation.' *Evaluation,* 15(3): 263–283.

Burton, S. (2006) ' "Over to You": Group Work to Help Pupils Avoid
School Exclusion.' *Educational Psychology in Practice,* 22(3): 215–236.

Candappa, M. and Egharevba, I. (2002) 'Negotiating boundaries:
tensions within home and school life for refugee children.' In E.
Rosalind (ed.), *Children, Home and School: Regulation, Autonomy or
Connection?* London: Routledge-Falmer.

Candappa, M. and Igbinigie, I. (2003) 'Everyday worlds of young
refugees in London.' *Feminist Review,* 73(1): 54–65.

Cantwell, N. (2011) 'Are children's rights still human?' In A. Invernizzi
and J. Williams (eds), *The Human Rights of Children: From Visions to
Implementation.* Farnham: Ashgate.

Carr, S. (2004) Has service user participation made a difference to social
care services? http://www.scie.org.uk/publications/positionpapers/
pp03.pdf

Chahal, K. (2004) *Experiencing Ethnicity: Discrimination and Service
Provision.* York: Joseph Rowntree Foundation.

Chambers, R. (2011) 'Relaxed and participatory appraisal: notes on
practical approaches and methods.' Robert Chambers Online
Archive, Institute of Development Studies, Falmer Available at: http://
opendocs.ids.ac.uk/opendocs/handle/123456789/603 (accessed 30
September 2013)

—— (2002) *Participatory Workshops: A Sourcebook of 21 Sets of Ideas and
Activities.* London: Earthscan.

—— (1983) *Rural Development: Putting the Last First.* Harlow, UK:
Addison Wesley Longman Ltd.

Chinn, C. and Malhotra, B. (2002) 'Epistemologically authentic enquiry
in schools: a theoretical framework for evaluating inquiry tasks.'
Science Education, 86(2): 175–218.

Christensen, P. and James, A. (2008) *Research with Children: Perspectives
and Practices.* UK: Taylor and Frances.

Christensen, P. and Prout, A. (2005) 'Anthropological and sociological
perspectives on the study of children.' In S. Greene and D. Hogan

DOI: 10.1057/9781137379702.0021

(eds), *Researching Children's Experience, Approaches and Methods.* London: Sage, pp. 42–60.

—— (2003) 'Children, Place, Space and Generation'. In B. Mayall and H. Zeiher (eds), *In Childhood in Generational Perspective.* London: Institute of Education.

—— (2002) 'Working with Ethical Symmetry in Social Research with Children'. *Childhood,* 9(4): 477–497.

Clacherty, G. and Kistner, J. (2001) 'Evaluating the Zimiseleni researchers' project: participatory research as intervention with "hard-to-reach" boys'. *Participatory Learning and Action (PLA notes),* 42: 1–5.

Clark, A. and Moss, P. (2001) *Listening to Young Children. The Mosaic Approach.* London: National Children's Bureau.

Clark, A. and Percy-Smith, B. (2006) 'Beyond Consultation: Participatory Practices in Everyday Spaces'. *Children Youth and Environments,* 16(2): 1–9.

Cline, T., Crafter, S., O'Dell, L. and De Abreu, G. (2011) 'Young people's representations of language brokering'. *Journal of Multilingual & Multicultural Development,* 32(3): 207–220.

Cockburn, T. (2010) 'Children and deliberative democracy in England'. In B. Percy-Smith and N. Thomas (eds), A *Handbook of Children and Young People's Participation: Perspectives from Theory and Practice.* Oxford: Routledge.

—— (2013) *Rethinking Children's Citizenship.* Basingstoke, Palgrave Macmillan.

Cohen, S., Moran- Ellis, J. and Smaje, C. (1999) 'Children as informal interpreters in GP consultations: pragmatics and ideology'. *Sociology of Health and Illness,* 21(2): 163–186.

Collins, P. H. (1980) *Black Feminist Thought: Knowledge, Consciousness, and the Politics of Empowerment.* New York: Routledge.

Committee on the Rights of the Child (2009) *General Comment Number 12: The Child's Right to be Heard.* New York: United Nations.

Concerned for Working Children (2010) *'He Is an Alcoholic, but He Is My Father', a Process Document on Children's Study on the Impact of Alcohol Consumption in Their Community.* [internal report] July 2010 ed. Bangalore: The Concerned for Working Children.

Cook, T. and Hess, E. (2007) 'What the camera sees and from whose perspective: Fun methodologies for engaging children in enlightening adults'. *Childhood,* 14(1): 29–45.

DOI: 10.1057/9781137379702.0021

Cornwall, A. (2004) 'Spaces for Transformation? Reflections of power and difference in participation in development'. In S. Hickey and G. Mohan (eds), *Participation: From Tyranny to Transformation? Exploring New Approaches to Participation in Development*. London: Zed Books, pp. 75–91.

Council of Australian Governments (2009) Australian Government's National Quality Framework (NQF) for Early Childhood Education and Care: National Quality Standard for Early Childhood Education and Care and School Age Care. Early Childhood Development Steering Committee.

Corsaro, W. A. (1992) 'Interpretive Reproduction in Children's Peer Cultures'. *Social Psychology Quarterly*, 55(2): 160–177.

Cox, S. and Robinson-Pant, A. (2008) 'Power, participation and decision-making in the primary classroom: children as action researchers'. *Educational Action Research*, 16(4): 457–468.

Crafter, S., O'Dell, L., de Abreu, G. and Cline, T. (2009) 'Young peoples' representations of "atypical" work in English society'. *Children and Society*, 23: 176–188.

Crenshaw, K. (1989) 'Demarginalizing the intersection of race and sex: a black feminist critique of antidiscrimination doctrine, feminist theory and antiracist politics'. University of Chicago Legal Forum, pp. 139–167.

Creswell, T. (2004) *Place: A Short Introduction*. USA: Blackwell Publishing.

Crowley, A. (2013) 'Children's particpation in Wales'. In J. Williams (ed.), *The Rights of the Child in Wales*. Cardif: University of Wales Press.

Cruddas, L. (2007) 'Engaged voices – dialogic interaction and the construction of shared social meanings'. *Educational Action Research*, 15(3): 479–488.

Davis, J. (2009) 'Involving children'. In E. Tisdall, M. Kay, J. M. Davis and M. Gallagher, *Researching with Children and Young People. Research Design, Methods and Analysis*. London: Sage.

De Boer, C. and Coady, N. (2007) 'Good helping relationships in child welfare: learning from stories of success'. *Child and Family Social Work*, 12(1): 32–42.

de Jong, T. (2006) 'Scaffolds for scientific discovery learning'. In J. Elen and R. E. Clark (eds), *Handling Complexity in Learning Environments: Theory and Research*. London: Elsevier Science.

Delanty, G. (2000) *Citizenship in the Global Age: Culture, Society and Politics*. Buckingham: Open University Press

DOI: 10.1057/9781137379702.0021

De Winter, M. (1997) *Children as Fellow Citizens: Participation and Commitment.* Oxford: Radcliffe Medical Press.

Dee, M. (2008) 'Young People, Public Space and Citizenship', PhD thesis. Queensland University of Technology.

Dewey, J. (1933) *How We Think: A Restatement of the Relation of Reflective Thinking to the Educative Process.* Boston, MA: Heath.

DfES (2003) *Every Child Matters.* Green Paper. London: TSO.

Driskell, D. (2002) *Creating Better Cities with Children and Youth: A Manual for Participation.* London: Earthscan.

Eksner, H. J. and Orellana, M. F. (2012) 'Shifting in the zone: Latina/o child language brokers and the co-construction of knowledge'. *Ethos*, 40(2): 196–220.

Erera, P. I. (2002) *Family Diversity: Continuity and Change in the Contemporary Family.* Thousand Oaks, CA: Sage.

Fajerman, L. and Treseder, P. (1997) *Empowering Children and Young People: Promoting Involvement in Decision-Making.* London: Save the Children.

Farrell, J. (2009) 'All the right moves? Police "move-on" powers in Victoria'. *Alternative Law Journal*, 34(1): 21–26.

Farson, R. (1974) Birthrights. New York: Collier Macmillan.

Fattore, T. and Mason, J. et al. (2007) 'Children's conceptualisation(s) of their wellbeing'. *Social Indicators Research*, 80(5): 29.

Fielding, M. (2004) 'Transformative approaches to student voice: Theoretical underpinnings, recalcitrant realities'. *British Educational Research Journal*, 30(2): 295–311.

Fielding, M. and Bragg, S. (2003) *Students as Researchers.* Cambridge: Pearson Publishing.

Flare (2009) *Active Enquiring Minds. Guidance for Adults Seeking to Develop and Support Young Researchers in Schools.* Chelmsford: Essex County Council.

Flores, K. S. (2008) *Youth Participatory Evaluation: Strategies for Engaging Young People.* San Francisco: Jossey-Bass.

Franks, M. (2011) 'Pockets of participation: revisiting child – centred participation research'. *Children and Society*, 25(1): 15–25. (First published online 2009)

García Sánchez, I. M. and Orellana, M. F. (2006) 'The construction of moral and social identity in immigrant children's narratives-in-translation'. *Linguistics and Education*, 17(3): 209–239.

Garrett, P. (2010) *Attitudes to Language.* Cambridge: Cambridge University Press Textbooks.

DOI: 10.1057/9781137379702.0021

Gaventa, J. (2003) Participatory development or participatory democracy? Linking participatory approaches to policy and governance. *PLA Notes*, vol. 50. Available at IIED website: http://pubs.iied.org/G02106.html?k=PLA%2050 (accessed April 2013).

Goffman, E. (1969) *The Presentation of Self in Everyday Life*. London: Allen Lane.

Green, J., Free, C., Bhavani, V. and Newman, T. (2005) 'Translators and mediators: bilingual young people's accounts of their interpreting work in health care'. *Social Science & Medicine*, 60(9): 2097–2110.

Greene, S. and Hill, M. (2005) 'Chapter 1, Researching children's experience: methods and methodological issues'. In S. Greene and D. Hogan (eds), *Researching Children's Experience: Approaches and Methods*. London: Sage, pp. 1–21.

Greig, A., Taylor, J. and MacKay, T.(2007) *Doing Research with Children*. London: Sage.

Grover, S. (2004) 'Why won't they listen to us? On giving power and voice to children participating in social research. *Childhood*, 11(1): 81–93.

Hall, N. and Sham, S. (2007) 'Language brokering as young people's work: evidence from Chinese adolescents in England'. *Language and Education*, 21(1): 16–30.

Hart, J., Newman, J., Ackermann, L. and Feeny, T. (2004) *Children Changing Their World: Understanding and Evaluating Children's Participation in Development*. London: Plan UK.

Hart, R. (1992) 'Children's Participation: From tokenism to citizenship'. Innocenti Essay No. 4, UNICEF International Child Development Centre, Florence, Italy.

Hart, R. A. (1997) *Children's Participation: The Theory and Practice of Involving Young Citizens in Community Development and Environmental Care*. London: Earthscan.

Hatton, A. (2010) *Shallow Democracy: In Other People's Shoes – Listening to the Voices of Children and Young People*. The University of Sheffield: Unpublished thesis.

Hatzopoulos, P. and Clancey, G. (2007) *Meeting Places: Where People & Places Meet: Approaches to Public Space Management*. Surry Hills, Australia: Youth Action and Policy Association (NSW).

Hill, M. (2006) 'Children's voices on ways of having a voice: children and young people's perspectives on methods used in research and consultation'. *Childhood*, 13(1): 69–89.

HMSO (April 2011) London Child Protection Procedures. Available at: http://www.londonscb.gov.uk/procedures/ (accessed March 2013).

DOI: 10.1057/9781137379702.0021

Hochschild, A. R. (2003) *The Commercialization of Intimate Life: Notes from Home and Work*. Berkeley: University of California Press.

Holder, M. and Coleman, B. (2009) 'The contribution of social relationships to children's happiness'. *Journal of Happiness Studies*, 10(3): 329–349.

Horwath, J., Kalyva, E. and Spyru, S. (2012) '"I want my experiences to make a difference" promoting participation in policy-making and service development by young people who have experienced violence'. *Children and Youth Services Review*, 34(1): 155–162.

Hughes, M. (2007) 'Every child matters: setting the context for the "hard to reach"'. In K. Pomerantz, M. Hughes and D. Thompson (eds), *How to Reach 'Hard to Reach' Children: Improving Access, Participation and Outcomes*. Chichester: John Wiley.

Isin, Engin F. and Turner, Bryan S. (2007) 'Investigating citizenship: an agenda for citizenship studies'. *Citizenship Studies*, 11(1): 5–17.

James, A. (2007) 'Giving voice to children's voices: practices and problems, pitfalls and potentials'. *American Anthropologist*, 109(2): 261–272.

James, A. and James, A. L. (2004) *Constructing Childhood*. Houndmills, Basingstoke, Hampshire: Palgrave Macmillan.

James, A., Jenks, C. and Prout, A. (1998) *Theorizing Childhood*. New York: Teachers College Press.

James, A. and Prout, A. (1997) 'A new paradigm for the sociology of childhood? Provenance, promises and problems'. In A. Prout and A. James (eds), *Constructing and Re-constructing Childhood: Contemporary Issues in the Sociological Study of Childhood*. Second edition. Basingstoke: Falmer Press.

—— (1990) *Constructing and Reconstructing Childhood: Contemporary Issues in the Sociological Study of Childhood*. London: Flamer Press.

Jenks, C. (2005) *Childhood*. Second edition. Abingdon: Routledge.

John, M. (2003) *Children's Rights and Power*. London: Jessica Kingsley Publishers.

Johnson, V. (2010a) 'Changing Contexts of Children and Young People's Participation in Evaluation: Case Studies in Nepal and the UK', Doctoral Thesis, University of Central Lancashire, Preston.

—— (2010b) 'Are children's perspectives valued in changing contexts? Revisiting a rights-based evaluation in Nepal'. *Journal for International Development*, 22(8), Wiley-Blackwell.

—— (2011) 'Conditions for change for children and young people's participation in evaluation: 'Change-scape'. *Special Issue: Child Indicators for Diverse Contexts, Child Indicators Research, Springer*, 4(4) October 2011: 577–596.

DOI: 10.1057/9781137379702.0021

Johnson, V., Nurick, R. and Shivakotee, R (2013) Guidance on Children and Young People's Participation Training, ChildHope UK and Development Focus, www.childhope.org.uk, www.developmentfocus.org.uk.

Jones, A., Blake, C. and Petrou (2012) 'Inquiry learning in semi-formal contexts'. In K. Littleton, E. Scanlon and M. Sharples (eds), *Orchestrating Inquiry Learning*. London: Routledge.

Jupp Kina, V. (2012) 'What we say and what we do: reflexivity, emotions and power in children and young people's participation'. *Children's Geographies*, 10(2): 201–218.

Kaur, S. and Mills, R. (2002) 'Children as interpreters'. In R. Mills (ed.), *Bilingualism in the Primary School: A Handbook for Teachers*. London: Routledge.

Kellet, M. (2004) *Doing Research with Children and Young People*. London: Sage.

—— (2005a) *How to Develop Children as Researchers: A Step by Step Guide to Teaching the Research Process*. London: Sage.

—— (2005b) Children as active researchers: a new research paradigm for the 21st century? Review Paper 003, ESRC National Centre for Research Methods. Available at: http://oro.open.ac.uk/7539/1/MethodsReviewPaperNCRM-003.pdf (accessed August 2013).

—— (2010) 'Small shoes, big steps! Empowering children as active researchers'. *American Journal of Community Psychology*, 46: 1–2.

—— (2011a). *Rethinking Children and Research: Attitudes in Contemporary Society*. London: Continuum International Publishing Group.

—— (2011b) *Children's Perspectives on Integrated Services*. UK: Palgrave Macmillan.

Kerawalla, L., Littleton, K., Scanlon, Collins, T., Gaved, M., Mulholland, P. Jones, A. Clough, G. & Blake, C. (2012) 'Doing geography: a multimodal analysis of students' situated improvised interpretation during fieldtrips'. *Learning, Culture and Social Interaction*, 1(2): 78–89.

Kerawalla, L., Littleton, K., Scanlon, E., Jones, A., Gaved, M., Collins, T., Mulholland, P., Blake, C., Clough, G., Conole, G. and Petrou, M. (2011) 'Technical support for the construction of personal inquiry learning trajectories across contexts'. *Interactive Learning Environments*. DOI: 10.1080/10494820.2011.604036.

Kesby, M. (2005) 'Retheorizing empowerment-through-participation as performance in space: beyond tyranny to transformation'. *Signs: Journal of Women in Culture and Society*, 30(4): 2037–2065.

DOI: 10.1057/9781137379702.0021

Kingdom, J. (1984) *Agendas, Alternatives and Public Polices*. (Second edition. New York: Harper Collins College.

Kirby P. (2004) *A Guide to Actively Involving Young People in Research: For researchers, research commissioners, and managers*. INVOLVE.

—— (1999) *Involving Young Researchers: How to Enable Young People to Design and Conduct Research*. York: York Publishing Services.

Kirby, P., Lanyon, C., Cronin, K. and Sinclair, R. (2003) 'Building a culture of participation, involving children and young people in policy, service planning, delivery and evaluation'. *Research Report, National Children's Bureau*. London: DfES.

Kirby, P., Laws, S. and Pettitt, B. (2004) *Assessing the Impact of Children's Participation: A Discussion Paper*. Unpublished paper. London: Save the Children UK.

Kirby, P. with Bryson, S. (2002) *Measuring the Magic*. London: Carnegie Young People's Trust.

Klein, P. (1995) 'Using inquiry to enhance the learning and appreciation of geography'. *Journal of Geography*, 94(2): 358–367.

Komulainen, S. (2007) 'The ambiguity of the child's voice in social research'. *Childhood*, 14(1): 11–28.

Kumar, S. (Ed.) (1996) ABC of PRA: Attitude, behaviour and change, a report on south-south workshop organised by ActionAid India and SPEECH, ActionAid India, Bangalore.

Lamb, M. E. (1999) 'Parental behavior, family processes, and child development in nontraditional and traditionally understudied families'. In M. E. Lamb (ed.), *Parenting and Child Development in 'Nontraditional' Families*. Mahwah, NJ: Erlbaum.

Lansdown, G. (2006) 'International developments in children's participation: lessons and challenges'. In K. Tisdall, J. Davis, M. Hill and A. Prout, A. (eds), *Children, Young People and Social Inclusion, Participation for What?* Bristol: Policy Press.

—— (2001) *Promoting Children's Participation in Democratic Decision-Making*. Florence, Italy: Innocenti Research Centre.

Larkins, C., Thomas, N. P. and Judd, D. B. (2013) 'We want to help people see things our way': a rights-based analysis of disabled children's experience living with low income. Project Report. Office of the Children's Commissioner for England, London, UK.

Lefebvre, H. (1991) *The Production of Space*. Oxford: Blackwell.

Lewis, A. (2010) 'Silence in the context of "child voice"'. *Children and Society*, 24(1): 14-23.

DOI: 10.1057/9781137379702.0021

Lewis, G. (2000) *'Race', gender, social welfare: encounters in a postcolonial society*. Cambridge: Polity.

Liebel, M. (2007) 'Paternalism, participation and children's protagonism'. *Children Youth and Environments*, 17(2): 56–73.

Lippi-Green, R. (1997) *English with an Accent: Language, Ideology, and Discrimination in the United States*. London: Routledge.

Lister, R. (2007) 'Why citizenship: Where, when and how children?'. *Theoretical Inquiries in Law*, 8(2): 693–718.

Littleton, K., Scanlon, E. and Sharples, M. (2012) *Orchestrating Inquiry Learning*. London: Routledge.

Lolichen, P. J. (2010) 'Children as researchers and partners in governance'. In S. Cox, A. Robinson-Pant, C. Dyer and M. Schweistfurth (eds), *Children as Decision Makers in Education, Sharing Experiences across Cultures*. London: Continuum Publications, chapter 17.

Loncle, P. (2008) Pourquoi Faire participer les jeunes? Expériences locales en europe. Paris: Harmattan.

Loveridge, J. (2010) *Involving Children and Young People in Research in Educational Settings*, Victoria University of Wellington. Available at: http://www.educationcounts.govt.nz/Publications/schooling/80440/chapter-1 (accessed April 2013)

Lukes, S. (2005) *Power: A Radical View*. Second edition. Basingstoke: Palgrave Macmillan.

Lundy, L. (2007) 'Voice is not enough: conceptualising Article 12 of the United Nations Convention on the Rights of the Child'. *British Educational Research Journal*, 33(6): 927–942.

Macdonald, G. (1996) 'Ice therapy: why we need randomised controlled trials in child protection'. In P. Alderson, S. Brials and I. Chalmers (1996) *What Works? Effective interventions in Child Welfare*. Basingstoke: Barnardo's.

Mahon, A., Glendinning, C., Clarke, K. and Craig, G (1996) 'Researching children: methods and ethics'. *Children & Society*, 10(2): 145–154.

Malone, K. (1999) 'Growing up in cities as a model of participatory planning and "place-making" with young people'. *Young Studies Australia*, 18(2): 17–23.

Mannion, G. (2010) 'After participation: the socio-spatial performance of intergenerational becoming'. In B. Percy-Smith and N. Thomas (eds), *A Handbook of Children and Young People's Participation: Perspectives from Theory and Practice*. Abingdon: Routledge.

DOI: 10.1057/9781137379702.0021

Martinez, C. R., McClure, H. H. and Eddy, J. M. (2009) 'Language brokering contexts and behavioral and emotional adjustment among Latino parents and adolescents' *The Journal of Early Adolescence*, 29(1): 71–98.

Mason, J. and Bolan, N. (2010) 'Questioning understandings of children's participation: applying a cross-cultural lens'. In B. Percy-Smith and N. Thomas (eds), *A Handbook of Children and Young People's Participation: Perspectives from Theory and Practice*. London: Routledge.

Mason, J. and Danby, S. (2011) 'Children as experts in their lives: child inclusive research'. *Child Indicators Research*, 4(2): 185–189.

Matthews, H. and Limb, M. (1999) 'Defining an agenda for the geography of children'. *Progress in Human Geography*, 23(1): 61–90.

Mayall, B. (2002a) 'Conversations with children: working with general issues'. In P. Christensen and A. James, *Research with Children: Perspectives and Practices*. London: Routledge/Falmer.

—— (2002b) *Towards a Sociology for Childhood: Thinking from Children's Lives*. Buckingham: Open University Press.

—— (2000) 'Conversations with children: working with generational issues'. In P. Christensen (ed.), *Advocating for Children: International Perspectives on Children's Rights*. London: Falmer.

McAuley, C. and R. Layte (2012) 'Exploring the relative Influence of family stressors and socio-economic context on children's happiness and well-being'. *Child Indicators Research*, 5(3): 523–545.

McAuley, C., McKeown, C. and Merriman, B. (2012) 'Spending time with family and friends: children's views on relationships and shared activities'. *Child Indicators Research*, 5(3): 449–467.

McCluskey, G., Lloyd, G., Kane, J., Riddell, S., Stead, J. and Weedon, E. (2008) 'Can restorative practices in schools make a difference?' *Educational Review*, 60(4): 405–417.

McGinley, B. and Grieve, A. (2010) 'Maintaining the status quo? Appraising the effectiveness of youth councils in Scotland'. In *A Handbook of Children and Young People's Participation: Perspectives from Theory and Practice*. London: Routledge.

Mcquillan, J. and Tse, L. (1995) 'Child language brokering in linguistic minority communities: effects on cultural interaction, cognition, and literacy'. *Language and Education*, 9(3).

Meyer, B., Pawlack, B. and Kliche, O. (2010) 'Family interpreters in hospitals: Good reasons for bad practice?' *mediAzioni*, 10.

DOI: 10.1057/9781137379702.0021

Michail, S. (2013) 'Child-led research in the context of Australian social welfare practice'. *Child and Family Social Work.* doi:10.1111/cfs.12087.

—— (2011) 'Understanding school responses to students' challenging behaviour: a review of literature'. *Improving Schools,* 14(2): 156–171.

Miller, R. (2012) Towards participatory democracy. *Education Revolution blog,* [blog] 1 April. Available at: http://www.educationrevolution.org/blog/toward-participatory-democracy/ (accessed 1 April 2013)

Mills, S. (2003) *Gender and Politeness.* Cambridge: Cambridge University Press.

Milroy, J. and Milroy, L. (1999) *Authority in Language: Investigating Standard English.* London: Routledge.

Morales, A., Yakushko, O. F. and Castro, A. J. (2012) 'Language brokering among Mexican-immigrant families in the midwest: a multiple case study'. *The Counseling Psychologist,* 40(4): 520–553.

Morrill, C., Snow, D. A. and White, C. H. (2005) *Together Alone: Personal Relationships in Public Spaces.* Berkley: University of California Press.

Morrow, V. (2011) 'Understanding children and childhood'. *Centre for Children and Young People: Background Briefing Series,* 1.

—— (2001) *Networks and Neighborhoods: Children's and Young People's Perspectives.* London: Health Development Agency. Available at: http://www.nice.org.uk/niceMedia/documents/netneigh.pdf.

Morrow, V. and Richards, M. (1996) The ethics of social research with children: an overview'. *Children & Society,* 10(2): 90.

Mythil, S., Qiu, S. and Winslow, M. (2008) 'Prevalence and correlates of excessive Internet use among youth in Singapore'. *Annals Academy of Medicine,* 37(1): 9–14.

Nairn, K., McCormack, J. and Liepins, R. (2000) 'Having a place or not? Young people's experiences of rural and urban environments'. In The Proceedings of the Nordic Youth Research Information Symposium – NYRIS 7, June 7–10, Helsinki, Finland.

Nash, A. and Roberts, J. (2009) *Supporting Students as Researchers: Making a Difference to Your School.* Cambridge: University of Cambridge Faculty of Education.

National Science Foundation (2000) *Inquiry: Thoughts, Views, and Strategies for the K-5 Classroom.* Available at: www.nsf.gov/pubs/2000/nsf99148/intro.htm (accessed December 2011).

National Youth Agency (2010) *Young Researcher Network Toolkit.* Available at: http://nya.org.uk/dynamic_files/yrn/YRN%20Toolkit%20Dec%202010.pdf (accessed September 2011).

Newell, S. and Graham, A. et al. (2011) Child-led research: piloting the Today and Tomorrow Research Group. Sydney, NSW, Report Prepared for UnitingCare Burnside. Available at: http://www.childrenyoungpeopleandfamilies.org.au/__data/assets/pdf_file/0009/86859/Child-LedResearchAPilotoftheToday_and_TomorrowResearchProgram.pdf (accessed April 2013).

Nutley, S. and Webb, J. (2000) 'Evidence and the policy process'. In T. Davies, S. Nutley and P. Smith (eds), *What Works? Evidence-Based Policy and Practice in Public Services*. Bristol: Policy Press.

Oakley, A. (1994) 'Women and children first and last: parallels and differences between children's and women's studies'. In B. Mayall (ed.), (2002) *Children's Childhoods: Observed and Experienced*. London: Falmer Press.

Office for National Statistics (December 2012) Key statistics for local authorities in England and Wales. Available from: http://www.ons.gov.uk (accessed March 2013).

Orellana, M. F. (2009) *Translating Childhoods: Immigrant Youth, Language, and Culture*. New Brunswick, NJ: Rutgers University Press.

Orellana, M. F., Dorner, L. and Pulido, L. (2003) 'Accessing Assets: Immigrant Youth's Work as Family Translators or "Para-Phrasers"', *Social Problems*, 50(4): 505–524.

Orellana, M. F., Reynolds, J., Dorner, L. and Meza, M. A. (2003) 'In other words: Translating or "para-phrasing" as a family literacy practice in immigrant households'. *Reading Research Quarterly*, 38(1): 12–34.

Percy-Smith, B. (2007) ' "You think you know? ... You have no idea": youth participation in health policy development'. *Health Education Research*, 22(6): 879–894.

——— (2006) 'From consultation to social learning in community participation with young people'. *Children, Youth and Environments*, 16(2): 153–179.

——— (2005) 'I've had my say, but nothing's changed!': where to now? Critical reflections on children's participation. Paper presented at Emerging Issues in the Geographies of Children and Youth Conference. Uxbridge, UK: Brunel University; 23–24 June.

——— (2004) 'Changing cultures, changing spaces: developing neighbourhood spaces for children using community social learning'. In K. Ward-Thompson and P. Travlou (eds), *Open Space – People Space*. Abingdon: Taylor and Francis.

DOI: 10.1057/9781137379702.0021

———— (2002) 'Contested worlds: Constraints and opportunities in city and suburban environments in an English Midlands town'. In L. Chawla (ed.), *Growing Up in an Urbanizing World*. London: Earthscan.

Percy-Smith, B., Burns, D., Walsh, D. and Weil, S. (2003) *Mind the Gap: Healthy Futures for Young People in Hounslow*. Bristol: University of the West of England and Hounslow Community Health Council.

Percy-Smith, B. and Thomas, N. (2010) *A Handbook of Children and Young People's Participation: Perspectives from Theory and Practice*. Abingdon: Routledge.

Percy-Smith, B. and Weil, S. (2003) 'Practice-based research as development: innovation and empowerment in youth intervention initiatives from consultation to social learning in community participation with young people using collaborative action inquiry'. In A. M. Bennett, M. Cieslik and S. Miles (eds), *Researching Youth*. Basingstoke: Palgrave MacMillan.

Prilleltensky, I., Peirson, L. and Nelson, G. (2001) 'Mapping the terrain: framework for promoting family wellness and preventing child maltreatment'. In I. Prilleltensky, G. Nelson and L. Peirson (eds), *Promoting Family Wellness and Preventing Child Maltreatment: Fundamentals for Thinking and Action*. Canada: University of Toronto Press.

Prout, A. (2002) 'Researching children as social actors: an introduction to the Children 5–16 Programme'. *Children and Society*, 04/ 2002, 16(2): 67–76.

Prout, A. and Tisdall, E. (2006) 'Conclusion: social inclusion, the welfare state and understanding chidlren's participation'. In T. E, D. J, M. Hill and A. Prout (eds), *Children, Young People and Social Exclusion:Participation for What?* Bristol: The Policy Press, pp. 235–246.

Punch, S. (2004) 'The impact of primary education on school-to-work transitions for young people in rural Bolivia'. *Youth & Society*, 36(2): 163–182.

———— (2003) 'Childhoods in the majority world: miniature adults or tribal children?; *Sociology*, 37(2): 277–295.

———— (2002) 'Research with children: the same or different from research with adults?'. *Childhood*, 9(3): 321–341.

Qvortrup, J. (2003) 'Sociological perspectives on childhood'. In E. Verhellen and A. Weyts (eds), *Understanding Children's Rights: Collected Papers Presented at the Sixth International Interdisciplinary Course on Children's Rights*. Ghent: University of Ghent.

DOI: 10.1057/9781137379702.0021

Ravet, J. (2007a). 'Enabling pupil participation in a study of perceptions of disengagement: methodological matters'. *British Journal of Special Education*, 34(4): 234–242.

——— (2007b) 'Making sense of disengagement in the primary classroom: a study of pupil, teacher and parent perceptions'. *Research Papers in Education*, 22(3): 333–362.

Reddy, N. and Ratna, K. (2002) *A Journey in Children's Participation*. Bangalore: The Concerned for Working Children.

Reynolds, J. F. & Orellana, M. F. (2009) 'New immigrant youth interpreting in white public space'. *American Anthropologist*, 111(2): 211–223.

Roberts, K . (1983) *Youth and Leisure*. London: Allen and Unwin.

Robson, C. (2002) *Real World Research*. Second edition. Oxford: Blackwell Publishing.

Roper, L. and Pettit, J. (2002) 'Development and the learning organisation: an introduction'. *Development in Practice*, 12(3–4): 258–271.

Save the Children (2007) *Standards for Children and Young People's Participation*. Cardiff: Save the Children UK. Available at: http://www. participationworkerswales.org.uk/standards/.http://www.un-ngls.org/ orf/cso/cso10/children.pdf (accessed April 2013).

——— (2005) *Practice Standards in Children's Participation*. London: Save the Children.

Scanlon, E., Anastopoulou, S., Kerawalla, L. & Mulholland, P. (2011) 'How technology resources can be used to represent personal inquiry and support students' understanding of it across contexts'. *Journal of Computer Assisted Learning*, 27(6): 516–529.

Schmolck, P. (2001) PQMethod (version 2.33) [Computer software]. Available at http://www.lrz.de/~schmolck/qmethod/ (last accessed 28 May 2013).

Shaw, I. and Shaw, A. (1997) 'Keeping social work honest: evaluating as profession and practice'. *British Journal of Social Work*, 27(6): 847–869.

Sheldon. B. (2001) 'The validity of evidence-based practice in social work: a reply to Stephen Webb'. *British Journal of Social Work*, 31(5): 801–809.

Shier, H. (2010) 'Navigating the tensions'. *Children and Society*, 24(1): 24–37.

——— (2001) 'Pathways to participation: openings, opportunities and obligations'. *Children & Society*, 15(2): 107–117.

Shier, H., Mendez, M.H., Centeno, M., Arroliga, I. and Gonzalez, M. (2012) 'How children and young people influence policy-makers:

DOI: 10.1057/9781137379702.0021

Lessons from Nicaragua'. *Children and Society*, DOI 10.1111/j.1099-0860.2012.00443.x.

Sinclair, R. (2004) 'Participation in practice: making it meaningful, effective and sustainable'. *Children & Society*, 18: 106–118.

Sorin, R. and Galloway, G. (2006) 'Constructs of childhood: constructs of self'. *Children Australia*, 31(2): 12–21.

Spencer-Oatey, H. (2008) *Culturally Speaking: Culture, Communication and Politeness Theory*. London: Continuum.

Stainton Rogers, W. (1997) 'Q Methodology, textuality, and tectonics'. *Operant Subjectivity*, 21(1/2): 1–18.

Stenner, P., Watts, S. and Worrell, M. (2008) 'Q Methodology'. In C. Willig and W. Stainton-Rogers, *The Sage Handbook of Qualitative Research in Psychology*. London: Sage, Chapter 13.

Stephenson, M., Giller, H. and Brown, S. (2011) *Effective Practice in Youth Justice*. New York: Routledge.

Suárez-Orozco, C. and Suárez-Orozco, M. M. (2001) *Children of Immigration*. Cambridge, MA: Harvard University Press.

—— (1995) *Transformations: Immigration, Family Life, and Achievement Motivation among Latino Adolescents*. Stanford, CA: Stanford University Press.

Subrahmanyam, K., Greenfield, P., Kraut, R. and Gross, E. (2001) 'The Impact of Computer Use on Children's and Adolescents' Development'. *Applied Developmental Psychology*, 22: 7–30.

Thomas, N. (2007) 'Towards a theory of children's participation'. *International Journal of Children's Rights*, 15(2): 199–218.

—— (2001) 'Listening to children'. In P. Foley et al. (eds), *Children in Society: Contemporary Theory, Policy and Practice*. Buckingham: Open University Press/Palgrave.

Thomson, P. and Gunter, H. (2007) 'The methodology of students-as-researchers: Valuing and using experience and expertise to develop methods'. *Discourse: Studies in the Cultural Politics of Education*, 28(3): 27–342.

Thomson, P., Hall, C., Jones, K. and Sefton-Green, J. (2012) The Signature Pedagogies Project: Final Report, Newcastle: CCE www.creativitycultureeducation.org/the-signature-pedagogies-project (accessed 31 October 2012).

Thorne, B. (1982) 'Feminist rethinking of the family: an overview'. In B. Thorne and M. Yalom (eds), *Rethinking the Family: Some Feminist Questions*. New York: Longman.

DOI: 10.1057/9781137379702.0021

Tisdall K. (2010) 'Governance and participation'. In B. Percy-Smith and N. Thomas (eds.), *A Handbook of Children and Young People's Participation*. London: Routledge, pp. 318–329.

Tisdall, K. and Davies, J. (2004) 'Making a difference? Bringing children's and young people's views into policy-making'. *Children and Society*, 18(2): 131–142.

Tisdall, K., Davis, J. M. and Gallagher, M. (2009) *Researching with Children and Young People: Research Design, Methods and Analysis*. London: Sage.

Travlou, P. (2003) *Teenagers and Public Space: A Literature Review*, OPENspace: the research centre for inclusive access to outdoor environments, Edinburgh College of Art and Heriot-Watt University. Available at http://www.openspace.eca.ac.uk/pdf/teenagerslitrev.pdf.

Treseder, P. (1997) *Empowering Children & Young People Training Manual: Promoting Involvement in Decision-Making*. London: Save the Children and the Child Rights Development Unit.

TSE, L. (2001) *'Why don't they learn English?': Separating Fact from Fallacy in the U.S. Language Debate*. New York: Teachers College Press.

Tuan, Y. (1997) *Space and Place: The Perspective of Experience*. Minneapolis: University of Minnesota Press.

Tudge, J. (2008) *The Everyday Lives of Young Children: Culture, Class and Child Rearing in Diverse Societies*. Cambridge: Cambridge University Press.

Tudge, J. and Hogan, D. (2005), 'An ecological approach to observations of children's everyday lives'. In S. Greene and D. Hogan, *Researching Children's Experience: Methods and approaches*. London: Sage.

Turner, B. S. (1993) Contemporary problems in the theory of citizenship. In Turner BS (ed.), *Citizenship and Social Theory*. London: Sage.

UNCRC (1989) http://www.ohchr.org/EN/ProfessionalInterest/Pages/CRC.aspx

UNICEF (1995) *The United Nations Convention on the Rights of the Child*. London: UNICEF.

United Nations (1989) *Conventions on the Rights of the Child*. Available at: http://media.education.gov.uk/assets/files/pdf/u/uncrc%20%20%20full%20articles.pdf (accessed March 2013).

Uprichard, E. (2010) 'Questioning research with children: discrepancy between theory and practice?', *Children & Society*, 24(1): 3–13.

——— (2008) 'Children as "being and becomings": children, childhood and temporality'. *Children & Society*, 22(4): 303–313.

DOI: 10.1057/9781137379702.0021

Valdez, G. (2003) *Expanding the Definition of Giftedness: The Case of Young Interpreters from Immigrant Communities*. Mahwah, NJ: Lawrence Erlbaum.

Valentine, G. (2004) *Public Space and the Culture of Childhood*. London: Ashgate Publishing Company.

——— (1996) 'Children should be seen and not heard: The productions and transgression of adults' public space'. *Urban Geography*, 17(3): 205–220.

Venkatesh, S. A. and Kassimir, R. (2007) *Youth, Globalization, and the Law*. California: Stanford University Press.

Villanueva, C. M. and Buriel, R. (2010) 'Speaking on behalf of others: a qualitative study of the perceptions and feelings of adolescent Latina language brokers'. *Journal of Social Issues*, 66(1): 197–210.

Walsh, S., Shulman, S., Bar-On, Z. and Tsur, A. (2006) 'The role of parentification and family climate in adaptation among immigrant adolescents in Israel'. *Journal of Research on Adolescence*, 16(2): 321–350.

Walsh, T. and Taylor, M. (2007) ' "You're not welcome here": Police Move-On Powers and Discrimination Law'. *University of New South Wales Law Journal*, 30(1): 151–161.

Warren, S. (2000) 'Let's do it properly: inviting children to be researchers'. In A. Lewis and G. Lindsay (eds.), *Researching Children's Perspectives*. Buckingham: Open University, Chapter 10.

Watts, S. and Stenner, P. (2012) *Doing Q Methodological Research: Theory, Method and Interpretation*. London: Sage.

——— (2005) 'Doing Q methodology: theory, method and interpretation'. *Qualitative Research in Psychology*, 2: 67–91.

Webb, S. (2001) 'Some considerations on the validity of evidenced-based practice in social work'. *British Journal of Social Work*, 31(1): 57–79.

Weisskirch, R. S. and Alva, S. A. (2002) 'Language brokering and the acculturation of Latino children'. *Hispanic Journal of Behavioral Sciences*, 24(3): 369–378. doi: 10.1177/0739986302024003007.

Weisskirch, R. S., Kim, S. Y., Zamboanga, B. L., Schwartz, S. J., Bersamin, M. and Umaña-Taylor, A. J. (2011) 'Cultural influences for college student language brokers'. *Cultural Diversity and Ethnic Minority Psychology*, 17(1): 43–51. doi: 10.1037/a0021665.

West, A. (2004) 'Children and participation: meanings, motives and purpose'. In D. Crimmens and A. West (eds), *Having Their Say. Young*

People and Participation: European Experiences. Dorset: Russell House Publishing Ltd.

White, R. (1995) 'The forbidden city: young people and public space'. *Arena Magazine*, Issue 15(February–March): 34–37.

―――― (1990) *No Space of Their Own: Young People and Social Control in Australia.* Melbourne: Cambridge University Press.

White, S. C. and Choudhury, S. A. (2007) 'The politics of child participation in international development: The dilemma of agency'. *European Journal of Development Research*, 19(4): 529–550.

Widerberg, K. (2006) 'Disciplinization of gender studies: old questions, new answers?'. *NORA: Nordic Journal of Women's Studies*, 14(2): 131–140.

Williams, C. and Johnson, M. M. (2010) *Race and Ethnicity in a Welfare Society.* Maidenhead: Open University Press.

Worrall, N. and Naylor, A. (2004) *Students as Researchers: How Does Being a Student Researcher Affect Learning?* http://www.canterbury.ac.uk/education/protected/ppss/docs/gtc-pupil-voice.pdf.

Wyn, J. and White, R. D. (1997) *Rethinking Youth.* Sydney: Allen and Unwin.

DOI: 10.1057/9781137379702.0021

Index

DOI: 10.1057/9781137379702.0022

DOI: 10.1057/9781137379702.0022

DOI: 10.1057/9781137379702.0022

DOI: 10.1057/9781137379702.0022